A SCHOOL STOPPER'S GUIDEBOOK ON HOW TO BE A JERK

ALEXANDER DEWEY LOCH

The School Stoppers Publishing House, LLC

A School Stopper's GUIDEBOOK
on
How To Be A Jerk

Written by Alexander Dewey Loch

Legalese and (Copyright/Publishing)

The School Stopper's Guidebook Copyright © 2020 by The School Stoppers Publishing House, LLC. All Rights Reserved.

All rights reserved. No part of this book may be reproduced in any form or by any electronic or mechanical means including information storage and retrieval systems, without permission in writing from the author or Publishing House. The only exception is by a reviewer, who may quote short excerpts in a review.

Cover designed by Michael Azbill.

Edited and formatted for publication by Ben Wolf (www.benwolf.com/editing-services/).

The advice and strategies found within may not be suitable for every situation or, frankly, any situation. The advice is written with the understanding that it is either written out of context or is meant to be is satirical or ironic in nature. Neither the author nor the publisher will be held responsible for the results accrued from the advice/insight offered in this book. Enjoy!

This book is a work of fiction. Some names, characters, places, and incidents either are products of the author's imagination or are used fictitiously. Any resemblance to actual persons, living or dead, events, or locales is entirely coincidental. No raccoons were injured during (or after) the writing of this book.

Visit the website at www.theSchoolStoppers.com

(coming soon—if more people buy this, that is.)

Printed in the United States of America

First Printing: Dec 2020

School Stoppers Publishing House, LLC

Paperback ISBN: 978-0-9600563-3-0

Ebook ISBN: 978-0-9600563-2-3

Library of Congress Control Number: 2020919544

DEDICATION

This guide is for those who see what's wrong in the world and the possibilities that exist to fix it. For those who want to take a deep look at themselves while having some fun doing it. It's for the jerks out there who are caught up in themselves and need direction.

In short, it's dedicated to me, obviously, because why wouldn't I dedicate the How to be a Jerk book to myself? What do you take me for, a goody-goody?

Of course, maybe it's dedicated to you, the reader, to those who want to make the world a better place by changing the things they can. Sometimes that's ourselves. Jerks can have good intentions, after all!

The School Stoppers Writing Group hopes to donate a portion of its (meager) profits to charities its authors' support. These charities are primarily focused on education and children.

One foundational building block of education is access to proper meals. If you're hungry, chances are you don't want to learn—you want to eat! With that in mind, twenty-five percent of the profits that School Stoppers gets from this book will be donated to *Feeding America* for the first two years of its publication. Lawyers made us add that.

Now, this might seem like a gimmick to get you to buy the book, and that's cool with us but the true motivation behind it is that we can't write without a purpose.

The School Stoppers want to promote and support education, which given a name like School Stoppers sounds odd but it's true. We feel it's imperative to promote and support these endeavors ourselves, and donating that twenty-five percent is one direct way we can achieve this.

CONTENTS

Introduction/Explanation of Absurdity	7
1. The Way(s) of the Jerk	11
2. Fitting In vs. Standing Apart	20
3. Self-Esteem and Society	36
4. Groups and Organizations	49
5. Projecting	62
6. Ego	80
7. What is an Argument For?	98
8. How to Argue like a Jerk	113
9. Wielding Power	126
10. Screw Etiquette!	146
11. Not Being a Jerk Makes you a Jerk	162
Afterword	183
Bibliography	185
Appendix	189
About Alexander Dewey Loch and the School Stoppers	193

INTRODUCTION/EXPLANATION OF ABSURDITY

The School Stoppers—now that's a name that causes confusion, much like the title of this little gem. Why would we create a guidebook to help someone maximize their jerk potential?

That's a good question. A good question indeed. There are a few points—three, I believe—for the justification of such a book.

First off, the information in this book will certainly help you become a jerk, and maybe even a better one... if a jerk is what you want to become.

In these pages, we point out ways we tend to be jerks or influences that help us become jerks. You can certainly use this as a guide to be the best jerk you can be, and we'll be marking these road signs as jerk rules for your reference as we go

We hope that with this newfound knowledge you might take a different road, one less traveled, than the world around us takes. One where you can use this information to lessen the strain created by the jerks of the world, as well as understanding your own motives. With this wise and worldly knowledge, we can point out the jerks and call them on their actions or simply change our own.

The second justification is, sometimes we don't want to be jerks, but we just are. I know I don't always intend to be a jerk, but I can forget what I'm doing in the small hectic moments.

Other times, I admit I'm a jerk on purpose, I'm not above that. Perhaps in pointing to ourselves and readers, we might be able to adjust our actions. To "be the change in this world we seek," to use the nice catchphrase that Gandhi never actually said.

Lastly, and perhaps most importantly, is the reason the School Stoppers exist. The name is strange for sure. After all, school is important. It is a pillar of our social and economic foundations. Who in their right mind would want to stop it?

We function in the world because of the things we've learned in school. We have built our world on the backs of giants, as well as other bodies... The School Stoppers seek to promote learning for all, which is sadly not the case everywhere. We have to pay for that structure, and sometimes that structure creates financial hardships that are unmanageable.

I'll admit our name has dubious origins. In high school, I wanted to be a writer. However, I didn't care to write for the school newspaper. I didn't like the hours. So on the weekends, I wrote my underground paper. In the dark, where the goblins hide.

I'll remind you that I was a teenager, and neither my forethought nor my hindsight was developed to a large degree. Hence the name, the School Stoppers Handbook was born.

It was a cool name. Who didn't watch *Pump up the Volume* with Christian Slater in the 90s?

Anyway, I think I wrote about six or seven issues throughout my sophomore year, probably four or five pages long. I wrote some small current events articles and filled the rest of the pages with humorous stories and jokes. I think I even offered some sort of puzzle and a prize.

I put stacks of them in the bathrooms during lunch and hoped for the best. I'm honestly not sure any of them got read, but I got to write, and I loved it.

Flash forward twenty years, and here we are. To clear things up, The School Stoppers means something more, something new compared to the days of my misguided youth. The writing group represents, a desire for change and support.

We hope to support knowledge and the growth of education inside and outside of schools. We hope to stop or at least slow the ways that would push us down, separate us, and hinder our understanding and ability to learn about and from the world.

We've found that there are misrepresentations in this age of information we take as truth. Foundational processes we believe are the only ways of doing things, simply because we have always done them that way. We don't write to invoke a spirit of revolution but of evolution, understanding, and building a lasting future... that is, until our sun explodes and reduces us all to stardust.

One more thing, a point the School Stoppers name feels strongly about, although might not always model perfectly: Context. If we don't have proper context, how can we give insightful advice, feedback, or differing viewpoints?

We take things as truth at face value more often than we should.

We have so much information at our fingertips we are "literally" drowning in it. It seems every day there is more content without context. We must stop inherently trusting unknown sources and instead read and seek the truth, or risk spreading this attitude of "jerkfulness."

Context gives meaning and helps create a foundation that we can stand on so we don't lose our footing. The School Stoppers work to encourage that type of learning in our schools as well as in every aspect of our younger generation's lives for the betterment of all.

Sincerely,

Alexander D. Loch
The School Stoppers Editor-in-chief

"Never let schooling interfere with education."
—
Grant Allen

CHAPTER 1
THE WAY(S) OF THE JERK
THE PATH TO THE JERK AWAITS

*"The superior man understands what is right;
the inferior man understands what will sell."*

—

Confucius

What makes someone a jerk?
　　Well, honestly, it isn't as easy as pointing out one thing.
　　You could say jerks only care about themselves, but while that can come with the territory, as we'll get into, it only touches on the surface. I mean, we all care about ourselves more than others in certain instances and situations in our lives. That doesn't automatically make you a jerk.

The fact is, it's hard to get through this life without coming across as a jerk to someone along the way. That means no matter how much you try, you're going to be a jerk at least once in your life. You can't worry your little head about that. Sometimes it's good to be a jerk. I mean it's working out for me!

Sometimes it's simply a matter of mishandling a situation. Our actions spill over to affect others in negative ways or in ways that are *perceived* to be negative. Perception is reality... unless you have schizophrenia like Dr. John Nash in a *Beautiful Mind*.

Perception, while something we can work to control, is not entirely within our ability to mold. We can to a degree, control our actions though. This depends on how we perceive ourselves and the situations we come across. From our self-perception, we can control how others perceive us.

Regardless of our forethought, outward demeanor toward others, and intentions, people have their own outlook. This outlook is born from personal experiences and relationships that we can't fully understand. Even though as a jerk you should think you can.

What we can do, is better understand ourselves and our true intentions. In doing so, we can more accurately display and convey those intentions to others. Maybe in analyzing ourselves we find that we are jerks. I say that's great! In working to know ourselves, we can better connect with others.

And as jerks, this helps us get what we want! Others might even appreciate your candor. This little jerk secret might settle conflicts before they even start.

That is one of the core insights I hope you gain from reading this book. Be yourself. As jerks, you shouldn't lie to yourself... at least in all situations.

You should also accept that sometimes you will have to be a jerk to progress in this world. As non-jerks, sometimes we end up hurting ourselves and others more. It's a very complex and difficult problem. That is if you're not accustomed to being a jerk. My life is great!

A small truth about being a jerk. Jerks are not something people should be, but we all are. Given an understanding of how to be a jerk, how we became a jerk, and how we are jerks could help make the world a slightly less jerky place to live. To help others, we need to start with ourselves.

There is a quote attributed to John Lydgate that says:

"You can please some of the people all of the time, you can please all of the people some of the time, but you can't please all of the people all of the time"

It's true, you can't make all the people happy all the time, and why should you care to anyway? People shouldn't look for others to make them happy. That's what abusive people do. Think about that the next time you expect something from someone.

Here we are at the mouth of a complex cave. Is it better to be a jerk for the betterment of all mankind or not? This is an enigma that will no doubt begin to rage in your mind as you read through this guide for sure. Let's take a second to talk about truth.

Foundations of Truth

While this guide dives into the qualities and experiences that do make us jerks, it's important to start with a foundation so we don't end up running down too many rabbit holes. Tricky jerk rabbits!

Context. To start, I'll lay out definitions throughout the book before jumping into certain topics. I find it grounds us in a shared truth and might just prevent arguments on those rock-solid opinions/facts everyone seems to be running around within their grey matter these days.

Speaking of rock-solid opinions…facts. Let's talk about what I mean by Jerk.

Jerks vs. Assholes

It's important to understand the differences between jerks and assholes. Keep in mind, this only works within the context of this book. I've read articles that would punch holes in the fuzzy logic of both my designations and definitions of these words.

From there we can get into the relative definitions that we will stick to. Jerks always prefer relative facts over absolute facts anyway. There's more wiggle room. Write that down. These will be my interpretations, similar to the "true" definition of nerds vs. geeks which says:

Nerds are knowledgeable in a field of functional study, whereas geeks are knowledgeable in a non-functional field.

To clarify, a geek may know the history of the Republic up through the Battle of Yavin in Star Wars, whereas a nerd may know the history of France up through World War I. Both will try to bring those up in everyday conversations.

While this example could be disputed, it's a pretty good guideline., but we've fallen far enough into that rabbit hole.

So who or what is a jerk? Well, let's start with the official definition and adjust it. Webster has this to say about a jerk:

"An annoyingly stupid or foolish person"

As well as this definition:

"An unlikeable person especially: one who is cruel, rude, or small-minded."

On top of that, jerk is also a verb that means:

"A single quick motion of short duration, a sudden jerk; gave the handle a jerk"

As well as:

"Jolting, bouncing, or thrusting motions"

By contrast, Webster defines an asshole as:

"A stupid, annoying, or detestable person"

You could say nobody *wants* to be a jerk or an asshole, yet the world seems to be full of them. Many people secretly enjoy being jerks and assholes. They could be categorically seen as more assertive in their personality types while simultaneously being viewed as weak in personal growth.

I say there's no reason you can't have both assertiveness and growth and this guide can help!

We'll use the following definitions for the duration of the time we have together.

The definition that follows, and thus the book's scope, will focus on this aspect of a jerk.

A jerk is someone who, while perhaps perceived as stupid, foolish, rude, or small-minded, simply works to better themselves or their situation above the situations of others, at the expense of others up to the point of harm but no further.

An asshole is someone who works to better themselves or their situation above the situation of others, at the expense of others even past the point of harm.

Harm, thankfully, is a pretty straightforward definition, and I believe it is a distinguishing line between the two. While a jerk may cause harm, it is non-intentional, or not meant to be lasting. That doesn't mean they shouldn't be faulted, mind you; it just means their intentions were not focused on harm but rather self-centeredness.

These definitions will help us understand how we can see such prevalent "jerkish" attitudes as well as policies in our world and within the context of this book. These definitions will help not only ground us but will give us something to work from and build upon. If we don't start with a rock-solid foundation, we can't hope to achieve our jerkish dreams of giving noogies to everyone!

My Expert Advice and Guidance

Like the great philosophers who came before me (Socrates, Plato, John Locke, Kant, Kierkegaard, Lewis Black), I think a lot and read a lot. I've even written this book because I have something to say and I hear famous people get discounts on crunchy tacos!

Regardless of my selfish pursuit of fame and eternal glory as well as the deep, intelligent thoughts that line these pages, I want to remind you to think for yourself. We read so much on the internet nowadays, but we don't have time to read the source material. We take things at face value even though we all know we shouldn't judge a book by its cover.

While I have to admit, through my humbleness, that I do tend to have rock-solid reasoning. I think it's important to note that this book is filled with my impression of things. That impression or view might be wrong for certain situations that you or others find yourselves in.

To state it plainly, it's not a one-size-fits-all. The ideas in this book are, on the outset, something to make you think and perhaps later implement positively. Of course, thinking I'm right and agreeing with me will definitely set you on the path to being a jerk in no time!

I'm not advocating relativism here as a common jerk you meet online might. Everyone does not have a "truth". There are certain truths, but relativism leads us down a wide path to a potentially impregnable image of self that, in my opinion, is terrifying.

Now, of course, if you would like me to start a cult following to spread my expertise and truth, you can reach out with your bank account information and I'll consider it.

Enjoy this book for what it is: a guide through the absurdity of some of the aspects of our being we rarely give thought to, but which affect and impact us greatly every single day. Perhaps if we gave them more thought, we'd be better for it. Whatever path you chose, keep moving forward... unless it's a bad path, then keep looking.

Society, Nature, and its Contribution to Your Path to Jerkitude

People suck. Well, the saying goes, "mean people suck." That's something we can probably agree on.

I like people though. I enjoy spending time with family and friends. I enjoy meeting new people. I like people. However, that doesn't change my view of the vastness of our unbridled potential and failings.

People are mean. Case in point, the infamous Stanford Prison Experiment—the one where the students were placed in a room structured as a prison, either as guards or prisoners. The experiment I'll admit is under some scrutiny as the results have not been reproduced.

It did, however, seem to point to how mean people can become. Reproducing such an experiment would be seen as inhumane. Perhaps you ask if the experiment doesn't seem to hold up under scrutiny why bring it up when talking about how mean people can get? Cause I'm a jerk and rational, even if objected to still has merit for a jerk!

While you may still disagree and say people are intrinsically good, the Stanford experiment does provide some corroborating evidence for my next example. I want to help make clear that many in our society more easily bend their attitude toward, well, jerkitude.

I can point to two modern performance art pieces from Shia LaBeouf and Marina Abramovic that shows how people's behavior changes over time for the worse. If we look at Shia's performance art piece

#IAMSORRY, we find that some of the people went to dark extremes when allowed to do anything they wanted to the actor. He was allegedly whipped and raped during the piece.

For Marina's "Rhythm 0" piece, we also can see a degradation in people allowed to do anything they want. Marina gave the audience items laid out on a table, ranging from feathers and flowers to a gun and a bullet. The audience started out timid, using feathers, but over the course of the six hours, their actions grew darker. Marina's clothes were cut from her body, she suffered cuts to her neck. The gun was actually pointed at her before a good Samaritan took it away.

You can see where I can say based on these examples our actions and attitudes do not tend to have an upward slope without action and rules. Some become indifferent, while other behavior gets darker.

You don't have to agree that our nature tends toward the darker gray palette than the lighter side, but I could bring up multiple events in our history you would need to refute. We do kill a lot of each other, after all.

One thing that stops us from sinking into chaotic self-loathing and madness is the law. Our laws help to guide our behavior. Granted, I don't know all the laws, but I don't speed, don't steal, and will absolutely never kill anyone. We all know not to tear off the label on a mattress we don't own, even if we really, really want to, because it could land us in jail for 5 years.

Those ones, I know. So, I don't do those—or at least not the killing, defacing mattresses, and stealing. Our laws help us to know what's allowed. Most of us operate within the law. And if there isn't a law against it, given this naturally downward slope I've pointed out, it seems anything is fair game.

You could argue against us being naturally selfish. You could look past the shoddy experiment and the performance art I mentioned. Past the groupthink and herd mentality. Past the social pressures that produce anxiety, confusion, stress, and anger, that drive us toward or away from society. Past much of the major violent events throughout history, saying it's not naturally occurring.

You could say it's misguidance that has led us to the point of harming others for our own gain. You could point out that some people demonstrate altruistic tendencies in trying events. I would agree with you there, but it just supports my point.

I would argue that these altruistic people have a set of internal situational laws or the rules they guided by. Some people call these ethics and morals. My point is, if you take those laws, those rules away, naturally, it creates a downward slope. Not everyone has such a solid internal foundation.

I'm saying with our laws, people tend to suck a little less than they naturally would. I still consider that some people only follow the rules because they have to, and this is a type of self-preservation and can't be pointed at as an inner sense of noble intention.

Wow, that kinda was dark…. What can we do about this downward spiral? If people naturally suck, inside and outside of societal groups, what is there to do?

My hope is that this is one of the benefits of this book. The jerk rules provided lay out some of our natural thoughts. Some are absurd when we analyze them, but being able to point out a rule gives us a balance. The balance between being a proper jerk and an outright asshole. If you recall, harm is where that line falls.

While I can't hope to fix the nature of humanity, we do need to have a proper jerkitiude. The unreliable teacher that the world is caters to this selfish nature, but this destroys our ability to achieve greatness. We're after jerk greatness here. This guide analyzes our thoughts and points out rules to help. It will help you on your path to a proper jerkitiude. It's not easy being a jerk and I'm here to guide you.

You're Welcome!

The Summaries

The biggest take away from this chapter is you're gonna learn how we can be jerks, and why we are sometimes. We want to give a foundation for context of what it means to be a jerk and so drew the line between being a jerk and an asshole at intentional harm.

I discussed a little about our nature and how left to our own devices how self-destructive we might be. Given rules, however, we might be able to lessen the effect of our nature.

One Last Note! Jerk Rules Found in this Book

I almost forgot to mention this. There are a lot, and I mean a *lot* of Jerk Rules. I think there are 365 in the ancient scrolls I found in Rasputin's Cave in Albuquerque. They coincidently match up nicely with the School Stoppers' other book, *365 Days of Terrible Advice*, also available anywhere Amazon sells books!

I could copy all the rules down from those scrolls and simply give them to you here but I want to focus on the rules that will best help you on your way to becoming a jerk. So while this book won't provide a complete listing, I'll mark the ones I use down at the end of the chapters.

I've found we don't consciously think of these rules as we go about our day-to-day lives, for good or bad. You can think of these as quick pick-me-ups when you're feeling a little too "goody-goody".

And now for the pride and prejudice... er, joy of being a jerk.

Jerk Rules

BONUS Jerk Rule #38: If you can reuse someone's work to make your work easier, always do it. **Pitfall:** This could be viewed as a proper work/time saver technique when done sparingly. Remember, as a jerk, your motivation is for your benefit, not others!

BONUS Jerk Rule #45: If you can make something simple seem complicated, do it. **Pitfall:** Some might label you as an expert in your field. Be careful! That's when other experts come to gnaw at your ideas, like rats eating wood! (Do rats eat wood? Who cares it's poetic sounding!)

Now without beating the bear, let's take a look at how you can maximize your jerkiness!

CHAPTER 2

FITTING IN VS. STANDING APART

*"Two roads diverged in a yellow wood,
But the road to becoming a jerk has many paths."*

Abraham Lincoln (probably)

So how does one become a jerk in life? Were the BeeGees right? Have we been jerked around since we were born? Is it purposeful? Is it a slippery slope, perhaps inevitable in this world? Has the inundation of information made us numb to insight?

Are we jerks because we just don't know what to do? As we hear about things that happen in far off places, do our eyes fill with indifference because of a feeling of insignificance?

We'll explore these ideas throughout this book, but we need to start somewhere. If you're going to be a proper jerk, you need someone else to blame. And where is there a better place to start than with your parents?

Growing Up

Growing up is one thing we all have in common. We all grow up, except for that jerk Peter Pan, why won't share the wealth? For most of us, we grow up, at least in terms of age if not maturity. While some of us don't mature (and that is a very helpful skill in the art of being a jerk), let's put a pin in that group of people for a bit.

We are molded from the very beginning of our lives. When we come out or into this life, a poetic person would say, we're tabula rasa or a blank slate. Well let me tell you, we're jerks when we come out.

Yeah, I said it: Babies are jerks.

Perhaps they're bundles of joy, they have that new baby car smell, but they're also bundles of natural selfishness. Crying, yelling, wanting food right off the bat. We are very demanding, and we don't care about anything else. Perfect jerks. If you want a jerk mentor, a sage if you will, watch a baby.

When the stork drops us off, if we're lucky, we get parents who care about our wellbeing. As it turns out, many parents can be jerks too, so getting a pair who aren't is something of a blessing. Given how we start out compounding all that jerk attitude (Jerkitude - TM pending) into one family, helps makes us bigger jerks or have extra potential. So, you might be at the front of the class already if you had jerky parents!

During your first few years, we only interact with our parents. Learning from the things they do and emulating their behavior. Babies might as well be little hawks. They watch everything. Parents don't seem to remember that. I'm guessing it's because babies are jerks and make parent's minds turn to mush sometimes. We pick up many of our traits from our parents this way. If they happen to say or do something, chances are, we will too.

As we start to grow up, we continue to listen to our parents. When they talk to us and even when they don't. I want to drive this point home; kids listen to *everything*.

If you have children, I'm sure many of you have experienced that moment in the car when you say something to another driver in anger, and then a tiny voice from the back seat repeats your words.

The situation goes something like this: You get cut off in traffic and pop off some long rant at the offender. As if by some miraculous force, your bundle of love and joy repeats only one word, whatever curse word you yelled. Nothing else, just the meaty part of your vocabulary. It's as if Loki himself came down and whispered in your little angel's ear. "Say this word, it's the only important word. Repeat it everywhere you go, in front of others. A lot."

I mean seriously, how do babies just know what the bad words are in a sentence? I told ya already. THEY'RE JERKS, that's how.

Even though your little angel is now growing a tail, it is a teaching moment. Just about every moment is an opportunity to guide us down one path or another. This is a foundational jerk moment. Do you remember the first time you saw your parents being jerks?

That brings up a good jerk rule. Rule #284, if you want to help your kids be better jerks. Start teaching them as young as possible the ways of the jerk.

After picking up our foundational word set from our parents, we continue to move along the path of the jerk and we find ourselves seeking other relationships. Usually, these are in the form of friendships or siblings. We end up making friends at school, some say school is a microcosm of society at large. But it's really a perfect breeding ground for jerks.

John Dewey tried to instill this microcosm more closely in his 1899 *The School and Society* lectures by better connecting schools with real-world applications. That's where we got ideas like home economics and shop class. I'm guessing vocational schools were born out of his ideas to an extent.

Thankfully society has corrected this appalling pigeon-holing of gender training. As a gift for the jerks in training, society took a rule from our book, Jerk Rule #17 - Over Correcting and catastrophizing solve problems faster!

This overcorrection as stripped out teaching rudimentary life skills in favor of skills for college life! Allowing the world to grab hold and teach us (and what a wonderful teacher it is!) how to manage and thrive in this life. This has produced a sense of confusion, anxiety, and helplessness that has given us jerks a perfect playground for self-involvement and fulfilling shallow satisfactions!

As a side note on jerk history, Melvil Dewy, a known jerk, created the Dewy Decimal System.

Schools are where we learned about fitting in and being isolated. Perfect Petri dishes. We learned what lurks in the hearts of humankind, both the bad and the good. It's where we might have gotten our first taste of life, filled with parties, popularity, and puppy love. It's where we gained lifelong friendships or learned we never wanted to speak to any of those people ever again!

It's in this truly foundational and important time that we learned to pick up new social and manipulation skills from those around us. We recognized what those skills felt like. Either learning from interactions, that we didn't want to use those skills, or we put them in our pocket to "pay it forward" as we grow.

It's quite interesting how little we as a society properly manage the connections and relationships of kids in our school systems, knowing how greatly these events can affect children. The world is truly at our fingertips, and there is no gatekeeper standing guard. Not to worry I am here to guide the way!

Not that there could be a guard to lock these events out. Our parents have to take time to utilize those teachable moments or our worldviews will be shaped by these interactions in a bubble. Perhaps a search algorithm will give our kids the answers they seek and whoever's making content that day. Maybe that's okay, but there are a lot of trolls out there waiting. #TrollsMakeUsGreat

Now, let's take a closer look at the dynamics of our schools and how this special time helps mold us into the best jerks we can be, regardless of the path we take. Inevitable!

The Paths that Lead to One Path

On either side of the popularity, fence exists wide entrances and broad avenues to becoming a jerk. We all have a desire to be wanted, needed, or have a chance to feel like we belong. That's a life secret there. This secret even applies to those hard bodies who say they're "over it" or "don't need anybody." They're lying to themselves.

I'll get into that secret in a later chapter. It's like "42" being the answer to life, the universe, and everything, but less complex and more useful.

Those happy few who want nothing more to do with people once had an itch to belong to something. This outlook stems from not feeling cared for or heard—pushed aside by the world, as it were. We can only take so much.

On the flip side of that popularity coin, it's easy to fall into the trap of picking on people. Heck, I would even pick on my friends. It's a form of endearment, right?

It's a tool of the trade for a jerk. It is your hammer. Your go-to tool. If you want to impress your friends, ostracizing and ridiculing someone has always, throughout time, been an attention grabber. (Jerk Rule #67)

How is it your problem if they go home and sink into a depression because no one likes them? They aren't popular. They smell bad. But that's their problem, not yours.

Life's hard. They need to learn that. People like learning!

This tool also instills a little bit of fear in your followers... I mean, friends. Nothing keeps people in line faster than fearing the wrath of your condemnation might fall on one of them. That's how a despot would do it, and if it ain't broke, why fix it, right?

Curious if you or your kid might have some of these tools in his back pocket? Wondering at the reason a child would have such an intricate understanding of condemnation and its effects for gaining acceptance?

Well, that's a psychology lesson for another book, but I imagine that it falls on two factors. The age-old argument of Nature vs. Nurture is over. Both sides fought, and it mostly came out a tie, though Nurture got a few shots in on the last couple rounds before the bell rang.

As I said before, as babies, we're intrinsically selfish. We can't talk, but we need things, so we cry for everything... as we should. I mean... babies, what else are you gonna do?

But soon we begin to take into account our actions and our parents' reactions to our cries for attention or necessity. In these moments, we're building a frame of mind for acceptance. As we grow, we continue to update this input, and it forms habits and understandings. It's all very connected, and it's something we as busy independent people don't pay enough attention to.

The Popular Path to Jerkitude
and the Unpopular Path to Jerkdom

In grade school through high school, as popular kids, we find that it's better to fit in than stand out. Better to be a part of the crowd than be an independent loser. I mean, loner.

Conformity is what we as popular kids learn we need. High School is like the Serengeti: if you don't run with the pack, the jackals will tear you up.

Speaking of fresh meat let's flip that plated gold coin to the bronze-plated side and check out what's going on over there.

The unpopular kids in my day used to be the geeks and nerds. Of course, the unpopular kids had friends too—unless it was that one kid no one talked to. I know *I* had friends, but I still felt a stigma, whether imagined or real, as part of the "unpopular group."

I can't say for sure what it was. Nerds would go home and study, eat dinner, do their chores. I'm sure popular kids did the same thing, but again, there was some sort of difference.

Unpopular kids had friends, but when they went to school, kids didn't jump out and greet them like in the movies. Unpopular kids were more concerned with a kid jumping out and beating them up. Unpopular kids had to deal with bullies...differently.

Don't get me wrong, popular kids have to deal with bullies just as much, but nerds and geeks lacked the social points to get others involved in stopping the bullies. Perhaps not being socially accepted can hurt someone's self-esteem? Shocking! Totally new information!

Nerds and geeks stand out. Perhaps they just aren't extroverted enough to fit in? That's an interesting viewpoint. Schools don't teach or promote group building or team dynamics like the real world does.

You might say, sure it does!

It has sports, and you know, sports, and then there are sports. Don't forget chess club!

The halls of high school were and are not the same for those across the popularity aisle. School environments reinforce the concept of independence for the unpopular. This leads me to the path to jerkdom for nerds and geeks.

Fighting off bullies and rejection constantly creates hard spots in us. Something we can pass forward as jerks later in life. It provides the foundations of Jerk Rule #23. All this rejection and torment has to create hard spots. It's not easy fighting to be seen or being anxious because of a need to continually hide from bullies.

Nerd life means running to class to avoid being pushed into lockers and not socializing in the halls. It means being shut down by that person you want to take to prom or being stuck in your head too much to ask for fear of being rejected. This is a good concept to remember, Jerk Rule #44. Independence means survival!

Sometimes, depending on our environment, the only way to deal with these events is to retreat into ourselves, our only safe space. That's a dark path. We don't need anyone, but it's one that also leads to becoming a jerk. Everyone is welcome!

In grade school through high school, we as the unpopular folk find that it's better to hide than stand out or fit in as it were. Better to be in the shadows than in front of the crowd.

Now I'm not saying you can't stand out in school by doing something worthy or interesting, but standing out from a crowd of friends is not the same as standing in front of the mob. Conformity silently preached by the masses. High School is like I said, the Serengeti: if you don't run with the pack, you better be a field mouse or elephant, otherwise, the jackals will tear you up.

Saying One Thing but Meaning the Other

Many social circles, from high school through college, even with being a "microcosm of society" at large, teach the exact opposite of what the world would say it wants us to learn. For whatever path you find yourself on. Popular or Unpopular. Conformity or Independence.

What could be different than being a part of the crowd or hiding from the crowd, you ask? Well, I keep saying, its concept called independence.

This word has caused confusion in our society and produced a fair number of jerks. The concept of independence feels freeing. It sounds "strong", like when I was a lumberjack for two years and I had to fight off the bears with my fists to keep them away from the logging equipment "strong". However, it's not what most of us were taught in the halls of our schools as we worked to fit in or hide from the limelight.

The Myth of Independence

It's with this understanding that we reach the notion of an important idea in and throughout history. One we hold and cling to. The idea of this thing we call independence. This notion, on its face, is an ideal that we all hold close to our hearts.

Being dependent or "fitting in" with a group isn't always the way to be, especially if it's one of the bad groups. Being independent means taking a stand, having people look up to you, having your life in order. Some would even equate it with leading, or "adulting" as the kids these days say.

But that's what the notion means, not the word, and that's where independence interlaces with being a real jerk.

Independence is important—no question about that. Everyone should have independence or at least a sense of it.

Don't get me wrong. If we could be entirely independent, I would consider that a viable option for us to pursue, but I've never seen it in nature. Not in one single instance. True independence doesn't exist anywhere.

It comes down to this: When we are in school building friendships and relationships, working so hard to fit into groups, these groups and events are important to us.

Some of us don't feel a connection. We don't feel like we belong. It's in these instances we learn this concept, most likely as a result of rejections or negative events over time. These compounding moments instill within us misguided self-assumptions. Either that we aren't worth the effort, or that we can get by on our own. Both are wrong.

Let me set my jerk cap down for a second and assure you—you are worth the effort.

The people who feel this rejection work to counteract that constant concern. We've doubled down on the idea that we are stronger if we are independent if we don't need others. We've doubled down before we even go out into the "real" world.

In fact, after school, we are given more "independence", either through finding a job or going to college. No longer are we confined to the small groups we knew in high school. We're introduced to a bigger, broader world. We're introduced to more ideas of being independent, doing our own laundry, buying our own food, not having a curfew, paying our own bills.

This is where the idea of independence gets murky, or perhaps a better word would be "conflated." So, let's look at the foundation, the definition, of independence.

What is Independence?

I mean, you have a pretty good idea of it already. We know we should be an adult, but is that having independence? Should we be using this word that doesn't exist anywhere in real life for what we are trying to obtain? I'm going to invoke Jerk Rule numero uno here. Let's change the rules.

As an adult, I have to depend on, frankly, too many things. I live in a house of cards, and I depend on others for just about everything. The bank, contractors, my boss, my friends—they all help me keep it standing. Perhaps independence is finding a job or paying your bills. Those don't exactly hit the mark for this grand idea of independence though.

I contend that not understanding or properly using the word/concept of independence helps mold us into bigger, more useless jerks than we need to be, and it's to our detriment as a society that we continue to allow this idiocy! We chase after something we can never obtain. I'll go into goal-setting later, but this misunderstood word ties into that tightly.

Let's look at the definition of independent as an adjective.

Of the three I see, only the first seems to fit. The second sounds circular, and the third deals with grammar. You can look those up if you want.

Who knew one word could have so many nuances? If it's such an understood concept, why is it such a complex thing to grasp? From some of the posts and tweets I've seen, not all of us do.

As a side note, maybe people should have to take a test to use Twitter. Something that tests your ability to do long division for those tough financial math problem tweets, and maybe a section on common sense. A breathalyzer app might not hurt. Drinking and tweeting can be just as dangerous as tic toking. See what I did there?

Under the first definition from Merriam-Webster, we see that at its root, the word "independence" means "not dependent" such as:

- Not subject to control by others
- Not requiring or relying on something or relying on others
- Not looking to others for one's opinions or for guidance in conduct
- Not bound by or committed to a political party
- Having enough money to free one from the necessity of working for a living
- A person of independent means

As children in school, we might grab hold of the third definition, and a few of the more maligned might try to grasp the second. Both are actually quite horrendous when you think about it.

I've already mentioned I don't believe in the second definition, and frankly, the first doesn't work either. The third and fifth definitions are what the world and the media talk about while at the same time promoting convergence for economic reasons on both local and global scales. That's complexity if I've ever seen it.

We commonly take the second or third definition with us as we grow up, regardless of which side of the popularity fences we're on. We crave to be unique and independent; we want to be noticed. We also want to gain friends or opportunities for networking while standing out.

Some of us build up jerk skills to protect us while putting people down or simply pushing them away. Others perhaps don't view young life this way, and instead of confining their worlds to treating people a certain way, they push themselves headlong into their studies and their passions so they might achieve their goals. Some would say they are showing an "independent" attitude.

Independent Jerks and Jerks Who Fit In

When heading out into the world after being popular or unpopular we strive for this thing called independence. Or if we're part of the beaten-down, we push ourselves into work so we can simply fit into a mold and no longer be the target of the bullies we once knew in the hallways. Hiding from the jackals like field mice... Ah, I love creepy poetry.

The paths to becoming a jerk often intertwine with the follower/blend-inners path too, but not on a level that has an impact outside of the group they belong to as a whole. And yes, that was a jab at conformists. You have to have your own voice to be heard and have an impact above the noise!

Some of us use our "independent attitude" as a shield in school to tell ourselves we don't need to fit in and have a bunch of friends or simply be accepted. We use it to say we don't care we're not popular. This creates those hard spots I talked about.

Hard spots help us be the best jerks we can be! What are your hard spots?

On the other side of that schoolhouse spectrum, popular kids *do* fit in. They have a bunch of friends, and for those children, sometimes after high school, things don't click anymore. There is a cliché in nerd films that the popular jock turns into the hometown loser. You know the one, Bob. (Sorry if your name is Bob, I meant a different one...you know the one Bob!)

We see in college or when going off to work that there are now a different set of rules, in the "after high-school" world and it no longer matters how "cool" you are. Although, being able to chug massive quantities of beer is still "cool" in various colleges and workgroups. When you're older, it's a "cool" way to get liver spots, but I digress.

Suddenly not being seen or understanding that change in the dynamic of "cool", can cause hard spots in these once-popular people. The world goes from saying to the unpopular "You need to be independent and work hard" to saying "You need to network and work with the team!", or for those popular kids who worked to fit in the world says "You need to work hard. Put your head down so you can get ahead." Confusing.

Confusion leads to aggravation, which helps us become jerks! We're on our way!

Our social systems also mold people into jerks by always changing the rules and not sticking to any standard. Jerk Rule #2! In the afterlife of high school, the nerds and geeks who depended on not fitting in find use for this "independent attitude." They pad their resumes with it and show a "go get 'em" lifestyle not hindered by personal attachments or hang-ups.

High school isn't like this for everyone, but the point to note is that the rules change. And those changing rules create a great disservice for many of our youth.

Pitfall! Changing Independence to Something Useful

I want to introduce another word into our vocabulary: self-reliance. Webster's definition of it is dishearteningly simple and only a portion of what I'm going to discuss. As an author and authorized Jerk, I feel it's my right to define or redefine words, even if I didn't make them up.

Webster defines self-reliance as "reliance on one's efforts and abilities." That fits somewhat nicely with independence's second definition of not relying on others, don't you think?

But let's analyze this beyond the surface. Self-reliance's definition is a positive assertion, while independence uses a negative assertion. This is important to note. Self-reliance gives us a definition we hope to aspire to —looking to ourselves—while independence gives us a definition we think we desire—not looking to others.

Self-reliance gives goody-goodies a definition where they can trust themselves, while at the same time reach out for support from others. The negative assertion of Independence works against this concept.

If we can't properly define what something means, we cannot hope to properly convey it to others. This confusion around the word "independence" in the different spaces of our lives hinders and infects our thoughts on how a person is supposed to be. How *we* are supposed to be.

This can also help mold our attitude when it comes to being a jerk. Since as a society we've tended to gravitate toward this negative assertion, that definition of independence is what most of us equate with being independent. This is a truly unattainable goal. No one likes being jerked around or offered a dangling carrot they can eat. I hate when my carrot dangles!

Ralph Waldo Emerson wrote an essay entitled *Self-Reliance*. Written in 1841, the essay is wordy, but one core passage pops out. *"To believe your thought, to believe that what is true for you in your private heart is true for all men, — that is genius."*

We should stop striving for independence and instead look to self-reliance. Even us jerks will get more use understanding this. If this is what we are after, young and old, truly at our core, but we don't know how to define it for ourselves or in conversation, we won't have a foundation to build on.

As a growing jerk, if you're battling ignorance within yourself, you can't help to win battles against the world around you. I'd love to give you bad advice, you should be independent as a jerk. However, understanding self-reliance is also a great tool to mastering the way of the jerk!

Let's mention a pitfall: properly evaluating these terms in our own lives could go a long way in derailing the societal efforts that make up the perpetual jerk machine.

Rest assured jerks, this is unlikely to happen as we would need to instill in our children a sense of self-worth as well as taking the time to teach concepts like "please" and "thank you." and virtual kudos from people you don't know mean nothing except potential dollar signs. And let's not forget that time-lost tradition of eye contact.

There's more to it than that, but as I'm trying to teach you all how to become the best jerk you can be. I'll be a jerk and leave you to your own devices!

Summary

In summary, I think (and let's face it, that's the only thing that matters. That's Jerk Rule #27) I've given you a few pretty good tools to help you become a jerk and avoid the pitfalls of that word that makes everyone queasy, "growth".

Before we close out, I'm going to give some quick bullet points to help you grasp the elements we've discussed so you can become a world-class (or at least a local-class) jerk.

Remember things don't change when you leave high school, or at least when they do, you should be upset about it because life is being thoroughly and disproportionately unfair to you. To be popular and to maintain that popularity, you should demean people because they are more than likely pushing in on your territory.

If you feel worthless, don't seek help or talk about your feelings. Instead, make others feel worthless too! Who wants to correct the issue when you can simply mask it? Don't drop this attitude after high school; you'll just command more respect.

Independence means not needing to rely on others, whereas self-reliance is a tool that allows you to understand your skills and abilities while simultaneously being confident enough to depend on others when things get tough. Now, properly ignore that savage/pacifist advice and look at some jerk rules!

Jerk Rules

Jerk Rule #2: If things aren't working out, change the rules!
Beware the pitfall: If you're consistent in your approach people might try and rely on you for things!

Jerk Rule #12: Everyone always has an ulterior motive, you should too. Never do anything without an end goal!
Pitfall: Having goals and a plan can actually help support others more than your own needs!

Jerk Rule #17: Over Correcting and catastrophizing solve problems faster!

Jerk Rule #23: If it was done to you, you should probably pass it forward. This gives you the upper hand over someone else! If you forgive, you're wasting that power! Better to spread the misery!

Beware the pitfall: If you forgive that other person, you may feel a sense of relief, increased focus on goals and tasks you think are important. I sense of calmness in your life. Weakness I tell you; peacefulness and serenity are lies!

Jerk Rule #27: What you think is the only thing that matters.

Pitfall: If you stop to let others give their viewpoints you risk giving them your power, don't it!

Jerk Rule #44: Independence means survival! The more you rely on yourself, the stronger you can be! Hide your weakness!

Beware the pitfall: Self-Reliance is the opposite of this rule. If you acknowledge your strength and accept your weaknesses asking for help you risk building networks where others are supported and helped over the needs of the individual. Your individual needs!

Jerk Rule #67: People love being made fun of. This rule makes friends. If they fear you, they love you! As a bonus, it can make you feel good!

Beware the pitfall: If you're too nice or express compassion, or *yuck* love people might get closer to you! AHHHH!

Jerk Rule #284: Generational Jerks start early. Who wants to be a *Toys 'R Us kid*, when we can be little jerks in training!

Beware the pitfall: Not being jerks in front of our kids we risk them being blind to the truth (Our Truth! *See Rule #43*) and being *gulp* a "goody-two-shoes"!

In the next chapter, we will discuss our self-esteem and how it affects us and those around us. After our parents and childhood friends help mold our behavior, society at large starts to push its grimy fingers into our clay. Glossing over this aspect and its impact could detrimentally affect our ability to be the best jerk possible!

Discussing how we can view the idea of ourselves within a social media society is huge. Hopefully, touching on these concepts it will allow you to step back and take stock of some of the things we worry about, along with what we convey to ourselves and others within it.

Remember, jerks need to take care of themselves to maximize their jerk potential. Let's find out how!

CHAPTER 3
SELF-ESTEEM AND SOCIETY

*"Sticks 'n stones may break your bones, but words...
Well, those get into your soul."*
—
(Most Likely) Richard Dawkins

One of the easiest things to point to on the road to jerkdom is your environment. That's the "nurture" side of that old argument brought into our universal lexicon by Sir Francis Galton.

I'm not saying Sir Francis was a jerk for taking us through it, but I think there is enough evidence pointing to the possibility. Most likely because of that discussion. I would say, *Game of Thrones* has enlightened us that if you're a knight, no matter how good, you're also a little bit of a jerk.

While I'm not a certified expert, I do a lot of people watching. Plus there was a study. Did you know that babies who are not held are at greater risk for not developing healthily? Neglected children tend to suffer from emotional control, understanding other people's emotions, and stress. Obvious, right? (Weir, 2014)

I disagree. I mean, someone out there had to perform a study to figure it out. A freaking study toe explain to people that it's better to be held! We aren't as smart as we think we are or would like to be. Or maybe that's just me, the jerk, calling the kettle black.

In the years before we are pushed off to school before we start engaging with the world and not just our parents, we discover our self-esteem. It develops from our "sense of being" in the world and the way we learn about who we are or who we can be.

We find this sense of self through those who raise us and interact with us. These interactions are crucial. If you want to raise a jerk, when they're young is the time to get started. Granted, you'll have other opportunities to instill jerk behavior, but there is no time like the present.

I could go into all the ways that you could pound on someone's self-esteem and pollute their self-image, but looking around at the world, I don't think I need to. Pretty sure that's been covered. Even so, it doesn't ensure you'll be a jerk, but you'll definitely be beaten down.

What I'll say is this: as children, we don't pick up just our parents' mannerisms. We listen to what they say, how they talk to us, or don't. How they correct us when we're bad, and we hopefully get our sense of right and wrong from them.

Let's back up. I'm not saying discipline made us jerks when I talk about "correcting". If we weren't disciplined that's a paved path that leads to jerkdom for sure: the "I do what I want, and no one tells me what to do" path. That said, punishments can also send a child down that same path. It's really a win-win for us if you think about it! Jerks no matter what! Inevitable!

What about the pitfall here? All those well-mannered disciplined children from the boomer age that tell us "whippin's are what made me who I am"?

Sorry, I had to stop typing because I was blinded by the tears of laughter in my eyes.

Clearly, some boomer children avoided the pitfalls just fine, but let's single in on the ones who genuinely do seem to have it together. People don't seem to be able to break down their arguments for a stance very well. If you can't explain it, it creates confusion.

For jerks like us, that's fine. Confusion helps us get what we want.

Whatever that might be. However, if "whippin's" are what you think is discipline, and what boomers think disciple is, then you're both wrong. So let me stop that train of thought now.

True discipline comes from a place of...well, that's where love comes in. If it's derived from any emotion other than love, it's going to be harmful.

Since it's important to create a proper foundation for understanding this pitfall. I want to point out that discipline from a place of love is not the same thing as punishment. Thankfully Webster would give us the way forward explaining that to enact discipline, punishment is required. Thank you, Webster! How else can we properly support the next generation of jerks?

Webster says discipline is:

"Control gained by enforcing obedience or order."

Or, as a definition further down states:

"Training that corrects, molds, or perfects the mental faculties or moral character."

I agree wholeheartedly with the first one; that's what our generation (I'm siding with the millennials and newer generations here) thinks of when the word "discipline" is used. The pitfall goody-goody people gravitate toward is the second definition. Although "perfects" is a little jarring, as that's a mostly unrealistic standard that is attainable in only certain areas and for short amounts of time.

To round out the complex "goodie-two-shoes" definition, it will help if we also look at self-discipline using the Oxford definition:

"The ability to control one's feelings and overcome one's weaknesses."

And finally, the definition of "disciple" itself, a word which normally has a religious connotation, is important to note. Oxford's second definition gives us this:

"A follower or student of a teacher, leader, or philosopher."

With those definitions, we can mash them together and find a more complete understanding of what discipline means for this older generation who we can't connect with:

"Training from a teacher/parent/leader that molds a student/child/follower's mental faculties and/or moral character so the student may gain the ability to control their feelings and overcome their weaknesses."

You can see now that "discipline" becomes not a fancy word for punishment but rather a path toward self-reliance—one that requires a teacher. Self-reliance is the enemy of many jerks out there.

It's a fine line between becoming the best jerk you can be and falling into a pit filled with lies these goody-goodies (who can also be jerks to us, it's all relative, right?) would have you believe in talking about aspects like, self-awareness, strength of character, and "growth".

By understanding these concepts and lies you can avoid such terrible strenuous activities!

These other jerks would have you believe that giving yourself a "time-out" to manage your feelings before dolling out punishment is better than unleashing your emotions. Counting to one hundred and going off to a quiet place isn't better. It's rubbish! Hot Garbage I say! Teach your emotions to your kids in the moment! That's how you teach strength of character and promote a proper jerk level of self-esteem. Random unthought out acts of emotion!

On a side note, if you are on the path to becoming a full-blown jerk yourself, don't force your kids to walk your path by observing your jerk behaviors. Instead, let them buy my book and read it themselves. How else am I going to make any money? Collecting Beanie babies only gets a man so far, you know?

Speaking of teaching.... I want to go back to the complex environment teenagers live in.

Self-Esteem and the School System

Our experiences of first through twelfth grade shaped the world as we know it. I'm not picking on our schools. We need schooling. We should be learning, and school, whether you like it or not, is one of the only institutions that we have that mirrors society before we go out into the "real" world. Or that's what we like to believe.

In truth, school doesn't properly "mirror" anything. The juxtaposition of life in school vs life after school is jarring, jerking to our systems. After school "Real Life" beings. That's a lie though. School IS society. It is real life, we only pretend it's a bubble as we transition to adults.

On a side note and as a jerk I believe that since harassment at work gets you fired, bullies in school should be given warnings. If they don't listen, they should be kicked out. Harsh words and harsh actions, but nowadays bullies kill people. They're assholes, not jerks. Real-life starts when you wake up in the morning, no matter how old you are. Come prepared.

Two huge factors that affect our self-esteem when we are young. Our home life, and after a short period, our school life. As I've said, I believe it's within these first few years that we develop our self-esteem or lack thereof.

Sadly, we feel it's only after this school-age we get the opportunity to accumulate things and head out on our own, but by then we've already been molded. Yet we think after eighteen is the time we should start learning skills for "real life". Before real life, life is a party and friends. Work and real responsibility and our future are what adults have to worry about.

As the self-proclaimed jerk let me do you a favor. No one will care about your future as much as you. Maybe you're mom, but it's still on you. Be selfish about your future. Rule #39.

There are two paths to a jerk's self-esteem I want to address. Let's look at that now.

Path One: Self-Esteem Unbridled.

Let's talk about the first path. Take me for an example. Even though I'm officially a millennial on some generational studies, I've always considered myself a "latchkey" kid and part of the Gen Xers.

There are two sides to being left home alone like Kevin in the Christmas movie where he kicks Joe Pesci's bandit butt! One, kids could develop bad behaviors, such as drinking, smoking, and being licentious. No question, I developed some of those behaviors as a teenager. Not sure I can equate them to being alone for part of my day growing up, though. The gooey parts of my brain were still a little gray back then.

The other side of being alone may have helped mold my character in good ways. I did chores, fed the dog, made something to eat, and did my homework all before my parents got home. I became self-reliant, resilient. Calm in the face of danger. A model citizen of the pre-teens and brat packs everywhere, if you will. I could make a hot pocket like Gordan Ramsey.

Something I didn't pick up on right away from being alone was my natural understanding of always being right. I mean, I'm still right on about ninety percent of the topics I talk about, eighty percent of the time. I just can't help it. I'm a genius! My mother always said so...

Although truth be told, it's important to point out my sarcasm here. I was a "know-it-all." Still am, right? How else could I write this gorgeous book? How could I not help my fellow reader soak up my ultimate knowledge?

As a kid, I wasn't given a lot of guidance, but I *was* given a lot of praise. That's good. Praise is good, when given in the right amount, anyway. It increases self-esteem, but praise unchecked and unverified can create arrogance, which is an important skill for a jerk to have! This is the first path.

That's not to say my parents always told me I was right, but I helped my brothers know how to play cops and robbers and G.I. Joe vs. Cobra to a higher degree than they could have figured it out alone. My parents were always around to tell me I shouldn't make them play a certain way. Can I help it that I knew how to play better than my siblings, can I?

Okay, so maybe I could have afforded my siblings more leeway on deciding how Duke shot Cobra Commander, but if I hadn't suggested building roads in our bedroom with piles of actual gravel from outside, where would we be now?

Thinking back, maybe, that was one of my ten percent ideas. My mom sure thought so.

Maybe some corrections would have been helpful for me. Perhaps I wasn't always right. I guess we'll never know until I invent a time machine. Maybe after this gem of a book, I'll look into that. I could, you know; my parents said I could do anything I wanted to.

Instead, I mostly recall how awesome I was. I got good grades. I studied a lot, and I had plenty of help along the way. All by myself. Perception is a key requirement in being a jerk.

Looking back, though, sometimes I got praise for things I hadn't even done yet or was only planning to do. But who was I to correct them? Their firstborn son, whom they love and adore? If they wanted to give me ice cream, how could I say no?

Which leads me to another point on the road to jerkitude: people can't simply put their minds to something and make it happen. If you're telling people that, you're a jerk. Congratulations! It creates such a positively destructive approach to life!

I'm not saying people can't come together and create near-impossible feats. I am saying it's probably something to note if you think you can, in your independence and solidarity, go to the moon one day—unless you're a billionaire – you might have a long row to hoe. Billionaires consist of the modern-day kings of this information age. They can do anything they want just about, and maybe for those like Elon Musk, we should let them reach for those stars.

The idea of "I can do anything I set my mind to" starts early. If we're praised for every little thing, it sinks into our being. I'm not saying you're not the next Einstein or Mr. Musk. I'm saying that even brilliant minds depend on others. As a jerk you need to know that... and shut up about it. Give credit, where credit is due. With you! Rule #216.

If you recall, independence is a lie and the idea that you can do anything you set your mind to acts as an extra layer of icing. The whisper of that idea can help make children brilliant and creative, but there is work to be done with it.

I'm not saying you shouldn't praise your kids or other people, but praise should be validated. If it isn't, it's just a lie. That leads me to a rule: Lying to avoid actual work is Jerk Rule #6.

This path of unchecked praise isn't finished. It forks, leading to more paths down the road, once "real-life" begins. That normally happens after college, by the way. That's something some jerk once said to bring someone down who had a degree and no cash because of the loans they took out to pay for that shiny piece of paper.

Real-life starts when you wake up in the morning and you need to be prepared. Time to put your jerk pants on and get out there! Now let's take a look at the other path.

Path Two: Self-Esteem Unrequited

You'd think I don't have much experience with this path because I just wrote about how I walked on the other one like a pro. You'd be wrong, though. I'm that good!

Unlike the path in Robert Frost's wooded forest, these two paths cross each other back and forth through the woods. You can easily jump from one to the other, depending on where and whom you're around. Jerks of a feather, and all that. Let's stick to our younger selves for the time being, before we were teenagers.

This path connects more with what I was talking about with neglected children. Even though you could make an argument that a latchkey kid is the definition of neglect. I personally found freedom and innovation from it. Maybe that's why I consider myself to be somewhat on both paths.

Neglecting is easy. There's an app for that. Life is busy, and we don't always have time to do the things we should be doing. Other times, we're just on our phones, scrolling endlessly without context or substance. "Connecting..."

While it's true that technology has helped us in caring for our children, who doesn't love the minivan with a movie player in the back seat? No more questions of, "Are we there yet?" every five miles—or at least not *as* many.

Having and utilizing technology isn't the same as being neglectful or abusive, though. At least not until the studies come out showing how it's similar and allows us to distance ourselves from people while remaining "connected."

In your case, I'm sure this doesn't stand out as I'm not talking about you, but let's ask ourselves, how often do we hug our children and show them valid affirming praise? How often do they hug us and not technology?

This second path feels darker than the one that leads to arrogance. Sadder. Not as funny as telling my brothers how to play. This path starts with a lack of *purposeful* interaction, not simply the normal interactions required to get through a daily schedule. Maybe it's okay to keep things on a surface level for interactions for some kids. I'm okay after all.

Some children have a strong sense of self from birth. I doubt it's good in the long run to simply assume that's true, but feel free to prove me wrong. It can help with that jerk level of self-esteem that I know I worked hard to obtain.

If as a kid you didn't get kudos for doing something you thought was significant, it can mold your thought process and produce a feeling that others don't see you or that what you do or contribute isn't important. That's good, it will help with your jerkitude later. The focus should be on you!

Not feeling worthy is a terrible thing, but it can be mitigated and molded! Sometimes that mitigation comes from putting others down. However, to know you are truly worth something proves harder if you don't have some sort of reinforcement outside your own mind.

Quick little PSA: You *are* worth something. I don't know you, but you *do* have worth. We are on this planet for a reason. Even if this doesn't sound like what a jerk would say to you it is a legitimate aspect of jerkiness but we'll save for in another chapter.

The Wonderful World of Worth through Connection with Technology!

I'm all for quiet car rides with the TV on in the back, but everything should have moderation to it. This might be obvious, but I'm going to talk about how technology shines a light on how we become who we are. We want to be jerks, not people who can't interact!

I said this would get dark, but it really depends on how we choose to view it. Keep in mind there are degrees to this as well. The "dark way" is a real way, but hopefully, it's one that can be avoided with a proper teacher. As long as our lizard overlords don't turn up the Hypno-toad scale we might be able to navigate the shadows of technology.

Our technology opens up the world in wondrous ways. The world, the media, the news, the marketing arms of every product that gets pushed out—we buy it all. These things make the world go around—because it would all stop if we didn't sell Twinkies and buy diet pills when we eat too many Twinkies, right? Nuclear fusion work be damned! I want my Tic Tok videos!

This economic machine shows us that being worth something means everything. Through ads and YouTube videos of influencers, it's getting bigger every day and we are told we've got to keep up with the Joneses to be worth something. either from our social media scrolling or the content of ads.

To that point, we can show others our worth by buying the hot items, echoing things we've heard, or snapping a cool moment on our phones!

The world guides us in its need to market and fuel business. It tells us to learn something (which is great), get a better job (which is important), buy a bigger house (which is nice), but it's an unreliable teacher. This can lead to having a life, or trying for a life that maybe we can't afford, either financially or mentally. It provides excellent help for bettering our Jerk outlooks!

As the world guides us to compare, technology is a window to see how other people are somebody and let me tell ya it's the glossy version. It's filtered for better light, and those filters are made for us to be somebody better than we are and get recognized. We need to follow along. If we don't, we could be neglected and not "liked," not followed. That's a lot of pressure.

We see in our friend's snapshot lives, what we think makes up their entire lives. That is to say, we believe other people's lives are awesome, and ours seem rather ordinary. Maybe we do pretty cool things, but mainly we find that we live to work. Despite that nifty little saying that we should be working to live around the office if we feel we're not, that we're doing it wrong.

That's a confidence booster when you feel financially strapped huh? I guess the van life people got something right, even if I don't understand how they take showers.

You see, we've created an environment of pressure by comparison based on our self-esteem and fueled by our comparative nature.

Watching television shows us how everyone's lives are richer and fuller than ours. While watching the news shows us how people have it worse.

How is it that in this world of opportunity, a nation under the new media as Green Day eloquently put it, we so often seek to escape our day-to-day?

Something fundamentally, foundationally, and intrinsically different in some goody-goodies out there is that they *don't* compare. Or, they don't compare themselves to others, but who they were yesterday and what they have done in the past.

Be warned, you need the fire of comparison to improve your jerk point of view. How else could you compare Bob's work ethic to your own? Bob's so lazy!

Rule #5 of being a jerk is to make sure you compare yourself to others. There is no way around this path to being a jerk, at least if you want to go on the Internet.

The pressure of comparison from ourselves and others helps build up our best qualities as jerks in training!

This can also manifest itself as showing us how much lesser we are than those around us and how much we need to improve.

On the flip side, we can show others that they aren't worth as much as we are! We might truly be able to understand that we're worth more if we have an Instagram life, and if we don't, we are lesser for it. Goody-goodies can't see the forest for the fire... er trees.

That's path two. Neglect in this technological "connected" world leads to comparison and isolation, and back to neglect! It's the circle of life Simba!

That was dark... and awesome to understand.

These two paths of self-esteem allow us to compare, and comparing helps us to be better jerks! As jerks, we can grow!

Summary

I've only covered a few of the paths to becoming a jerk but we've covered some of the broad important aspects to keep in mind.

There are two paths when growing up, and they both involve self-esteem. If you have a bloated self-esteem, born of praise given without warrant. Perhaps you've felt neglected, in both cases, you're prime for picking up the idea that putting people down will either elevate your standing or keep it high enough where people won't question your lack of work ethic around the office.

We went over how society gives us a comparative foundation that directs us to compare ourselves to others. I feel this is one of the most important, easy-to-say, yet hard-to-master concepts from this book. Keep comparing! It leads to jerk growth!

Keep comparing yourself to others, and don't compare yourself to who you were yesterday. There are some more lessons before you can fully utilize comparisons. I'll pick up on more utilization of this concept as we continue.

Remember, for my jerks-in-training out there, neglecting others as you have been neglected builds jerk character in both yourself and those around you! If you want to be a jerk, ignore others you love, and don't open yourself up and explain your feelings.

Also, know that this will help others become better jerks from constantly watching your jerky attitude. If you feel unwanted, you are more capable of making others feel the same. Continue to reflect how you feel about yourself onto others, and you'll be a journeyman jerk in no time!

Jerk Rules

Now for the main jerk rules we pointed out in this chapter.

Jerk Rule #5: Make sure you compare yourself to others. (The media will help you with this!)
   Pitfall: If you start to look back at your own achievements, you risk losing the fire that makes up the lifeblood of humanity and growth. Competition!

Jerk Rule #6: Lying to avoid actual work.

    Beware the pitfall: As a jerk, it might be more advantageous to let people know you just don't have time for them. Lying in itself means work!

Jerk Rule #39: Be selfish about your future.

BONUS Jerk Rule #126: Other people know what they're doing. You should expect them to guide you.

Jerk Rule #216: Give credit where credit is due. With you!

Now that we've discussed our upbringing and schools let's take a look at the broader world. What aspects of the groups we belong to affect us and turn us into jerks?

I know I only belong to the best groups, the jerkiest-jerk groups. The *crème de la jerk* if you will. It's probably the same for you too. Let's find out why.

CHAPTER 4
GROUPS AND ORGANIZATIONS
THE GOOD AND BAD THINGS ABOUT GROUPS AND HOW THEY AFFECT US... WELL, MOSTLY THE BAD THINGS.

*"Birds of a feather flock together,
unless a hurricane comes along,
then you see their true character."*

—

Frank "Ol' Man Tan" Tanner

In school, we get to understand cliques and social circles. Throughout our lives, we find various combinations of these groups. Many of which we will look to fit in with or stand apart from. What we learn while we're growing up in school is these groups can affect not only how we act socially and what we can achieve but they also play a part in molding who we become.

Groups are fun! They are one of the marvelous and actual ways we connect to each other. Forget FaceSpace and Instachat, unless you're in the camp of jerks that believe Jerk Rule #29 (people care about what you say) applies to these Internet groups and you're interested in how Jerk Rule #33 (people buy crap) can benefit your goals.

In pre-adulting life, aka the college years, you're introduced to a bigger broader world. Or maybe you don't want to go to college because you realize you'll be paying off that loan for the next 20-plus years, and having a piece of paper that says you're smart doesn't match the ratio of stress and debt bondage it would create. To each their own.

The rise in college tuition compared to inflation rates is making it harder and harder to afford an education without working for another twenty to get out from under it. Gotta keep those wheels turning!

But if college is not for you (and trust me, it's not for a lot of people nowadays), you can still learn something from this chapter. College/early work-life is similar to high school. Although the dynamics of responsibility start showing their ugly heads during this time.

You're probably stuck in a bunch of different classes/offices/working conditions, and while these allow you to meet people, you have more responsibilities now. That means less time for fun and hanging out playing guitar with your friends in the garage. Sometimes your friends don't even have time to hang out at the mall or the skate park anymore.

(I was a mall rat back in the days before Kevin Smith made that movie. I've heard the Internet is killing retail stores, but malls are still a thing, right?)

Your work friends have projects to deal with, kids, TV shows to binge-watch, or hiking somewhere for their health or wellbeing. Weirdos.

So while you have a group of friends and I'm sure you're learning great ways to be a jerk from their input with all the added responsibilities, time is not your friend.

I hate to say this, but from here on out it never gets any better. That's why our parents always told us to enjoy the time we had as kids. Even with the added responsibilities, there are just so many more opportunities and experiences that can help speed you along the jerk path. In fact, those very responsibilities might be pushing us closer to our goal of being jerks if we've managed to avoid such things up until now.

If you've decided to go to college, you've probably heard about these groups called sororities and fraternities. You might even have one earmarked for joining. These groups can be pretty cool, while others seem to have it all wrong. Still, some of them continue having ragers!

Take Zeta Beta Tau—they give out meals to homeless people in Venice Beach every year. What went wrong with this group? Did they not see *Animal House*? There's a fraternity from the University of Texas that helped raise 40,000 dollars for the SEAL Legacy Foundation, a group that cares for wounded SEALs and their families. What is with all this support?

But the issue we're touching on with sororities and fraternities isn't about the events they put on for the world, it's how being part of a group affects you. There are different aspects to some of these groups; they're elite. As jerks, we are elite. It's just facts I'm spitting. Don't be jelly. #EliteJerks

Let's not get it twisted—while some of them are creating helpful environments, the stereotype of a frat brother or sorority sister still exists. Thankfully! But looking past that awesomeness, being part of a group can help structure your time. They help you to succeed, push you forward. While we jerks should be independent, utilizing tools...er people, is in our blood.

Take the infamous Skull & Bones from Yale. This group is quiet, which makes sense as to why it's been called a secret society, but it's just another group. You can probably tell I don't put much stock in secret societies. So far, I think the only way to prove you even belong to one of these societies is if you become president and went to Yale.

Suffice it to say, I don't think it's much of a secret as to what's going on behind their doors. I mean besides the goat blood sacrifice on the fifth Wednesday of February every sixty-four years. Skull & Bones isn't harnessing ancient secrets; they are just very good at networking and, let's face it, public marketing. That's what a fraternity/sorority should be about: increasing your network. Increasing your network increases your chances of success. As jerks, it's all about us.

I don't mean increasing your social circle with the guy who can chug twelve beers in twelve minutes. He's not going to be very helpful in the real world, although he might be a good friend to flock with. We're looking at how groups can help you along in becoming the jerk you want to be. Maybe that means downing a case in an afternoon. You could be that jerk, but you won't be the one in the Whitehouse.

Although, it's important to remember Rule #47: be friends with people that will hold you back. This will help hamper your mindset in what you can accomplish. Although I have to say this is an Optional rule. Some jerks want more than just a high tolerance for Natural Light.

However, if you want to build a worthwhile network, jerk, or non-jerk you have to think about the future. A sorority or fraternity isn't just about parties or having some sort of status around campus. Although jerks should feel elite, even if it's only because of their chugging stamina.

Careful your pride is in the right place! Many college students feel pride in their accomplishments. As jerks, we should feel pride about who we are. I mean, that's really enough. That's a lesson born from Path one. High Self-esteem. There isn't anything wrong with having some small degree of pride for the group you belong to either. Groups can go off the rails into asshole territory rather quickly.

These Greek clubs were created, in essence, for networking. Phi Beta Kappa was founded in 1775. Interestingly enough, it also has chapters at Yale, and although it's not considered a secret society, I bet the connections it offers are similar to the Old Skull & Bones once you get to know the alumni.

Sororities on the other hand took off later, in the 1850s with Alpha Delta Pi. The development of these organizations goes to show one way that women were working to create equality even back then. That doesn't seem very jerky, but I'm sure they had to pull a few jerk moves to get setup. I'm all for that.

However non-jerky and well-founded these groups are, mainstream media/movies have made them into little more than places people go to party. Kind of a jerky thing for the media and Hollywood to do, even if it's true to some degree.

This brings me to a Jerk Rule #141: generalizing for the sake of an argument. (We'll discuss arguing later.). I have researched this topic extensively. I'm practically an expert now. I've been watching *Old School*, *Animal House*, *PCU*, and *Road Trip*, just to name a few. I found that the truth is that they are more influential than just helping us master the perfect keg stand—which, by the way, is harder than it looks. Thirteen seconds is my record to beat.

Fraternities and sororities do help with networking after college. Forget that some jerk said being part of a frat means you might not be a good leader. Their reach depends on how far their alumni members have gotten in the work world, and *your* reach depends on how much time you devote to utilizing those connections.

Jerk Rule #87 If you don't work the system, the system won't work. For our interests, this ultimately depends on following the Jerk Rules laid out in this book.

I believe this media stereotype helps show that even though we can respect our fellow jerks, some jerks just want to have fun. Some jerks who weren't included in the fun in school will work to ruin things for the rest of us. There's a lot of power in groups to wield so you should understand how to wield it.

So how does belonging to a group help mold me into a jerk? Well, it doesn't... not really. The relationship dynamics of the group will help with that. Direct or in-direct intentions are still up to you. Let's talk about some interactions in a group you should know about. I'll give you some examples in the sections ahead.

Groupthink

Groups and organizations aren't (ultimately) responsible for creating the jerks in the world. I can name a few asshole groups that stand out, but not as many "jerk" groups. Rather, we can see these groups in terms of having the potential to mass-produce people with jerk qualities. All it takes is for a jerk or a group of jerks to be involved. So let's talk about groupthink theory!

I'm not a psychologist in any sense of the word. I encourage you to learn more by doing your own research into these areas, but I'll at least give you an introduction to the topic. I'm just a run-of-the-mill YouTube zombie and wanted to give you a heads up that I'm not the "end-all-be-all."

Even though I really am. Trust me.

The name "Groupthink Theory" was coined by a guy named William H. Whyte Jr. back in 1952, and I believe he pulled the reference from George Orwell of *Animal Farm* and *1984* fame. If you haven't read *Animal Farm (written in 1945)*, read it after this book.

The groupthink notion was further built on by a guy named Irving Janis in a few papers, one being *Victims of Groupthink* in 1972. The way I see the theory of groupthink is, an outcome of peer pressure in a group, normally against the common good of that group or outside groups.

High schools are full of potential for groupthink. Groupthink is how they say "bad", but if you're a jerk groupthink can boost your self-esteem while at the same time affording ruination for the group's potential! Win-Win! Misery loves group thinkers!

Groupthink happens, or theoretically could happen, when a leader or leaders of a group have a dominant hold. The group has a strong, close-knit connection but lacks proper communication channels to disperse knowledge. A lack of standards that everyone in the group should knowingly follow. Finally, a "me first" approach to the leadership style makes a great breeding ground for groupthink to take hold of.

Just something to point out. I've just given an accurate representation of our two-party political and social media systems in America... I certainly didn't mean to, though.

To properly be a jerk, you should understand peer pressure, also known as a normative influence. What better way to understand something than to talk about it in a seemingly unrelated side topic! Jerk Rule #28 in practice. (More on that later. Just stay with me.)

> *"It is said that if you know your enemies and know yourself, you will not be imperiled in a hundred battles; if you do not know your enemies but do know yourself, you will win one and lose one; if you do not know your enemies nor yourself, you will be imperiled in every single battle."* (Tzu, 5 BC)

General Sun Tzu said that he gained this knowledge from life experiences and didn't read it in a blog. It's a pretty awesome quote and is pertinent here. It's important to understand peer pressure (your enemy) whether you want to be the biggest jerk or not. If you don't know who you are and what you want, peer pressure will beat you up.

Without research and introspection, whatever sounds best to you will guide you. And that my journeyman jerk is a dangerous way to live. As we talk about arguing this insight will be invaluable. It probably applies to "good-two-shoes" as well. Can't they just stay out of our business!

For the jerks out there, the more people you can convince that your idea is the right one, the easier it will be in convincing all the people. That's not an easy task, but that means all you need to do is work on your marketing skills.

In the last chapter, we saw that self-esteem plays a big part in our interactions with the world. How confident we feel is a byproduct of how we were raised and the environments we were raised in. I would even go as far as to say that the underlying drive for social acceptance is solely rooted in the confidence we have in ourselves.

Peer pressure happens when we have a desire to be accepted or liked. Note how groupthink and peer pressure tie into confidence and self-esteem. Confidence is the feeling or belief that we can rely on someone or something. That means self-confidence is our belief in the ability to rely on ourselves. As jerks this presents itself within the complexity of independence, as goody-two-shoes, it's in the positive assertation of self-reliance. Careful of that pitfall!

Self-esteem is confidence in our worth or abilities. Independence is not relying on others. The two terms are closely connected but not the same.

Self-Esteem and Confidence Concerning Peer Pressure Within a Group

Let's look at a concept that isn't peer pressure but looks at the relation of self-esteem and confidence. If my self-esteem was high but my self-confidence in understanding a concept was about equal or less than my confidence in a group's understanding of that same concept, I would be experiencing something called informative influence.

This is to say if I believe the group had information on a situation that I did not fully understand I would have reason to believe they know what they are talking about. In so, I'd decide to follow them. This concept shouldn't be confused with peer pressure.

Let's bounce over to normative influence which, again, is better known as peer pressure. Taking the same situation except saying I have lower self-esteem this time. I might be more susceptible to siding with what the group wanted over my own thoughts because of a lack of trust in my worth or abilities.

This could be true even if my self-confidence were high, as my desire to be accepted could outweigh my desire to do something right, hence pointing to my low self-esteem being the factor.

We can now determine as jerks in training that if we want to convince someone with high self-esteem, we're going to have to do some more legwork. Our ideas are going to have to be solid.

I must warn you, the path to being a jerk is not something to take lightly. You can't phone-in these actions. You're going to need to know what you're talking about.

If you're stupid, you aren't going to make it. Sorry to be a jerk, but it's true. Just remember "J" Rule #15 (You're never not right.), and you'll calm down. Being a well-to-do jerk is not going to be easy, but fear not! You can be a jerk without being smart, too.

Groupthink can be avoided, but first, it has to be acknowledged as a possibility. We need to know our enemy, and as jerks, that enemy works against groupthink, both on an individual level and as an organization or group. Watch for these pitfalls, you have to work harder if groupthink isn't present!

How can we, as jerks, support groupthink for our benefit you ask?

If you're a leader, providing your thoughts on a topic in a meeting at the very beginning can influence someone's decision to speak up or perhaps change their mind. This helps as you can possibly change their mind before they even talk. The group might not hear their thoughts at all!

Another helpful tip to promote groupthink is that after you give your vision and speak, don't open up the conversation by asking for feedback. You'll need to be closed to disagreements! If you can show you're not accepting of conflicting ideas using negative words and body language it goes a long way in stifling interaction within groups. As a jerk in a leadership position, you need to have thin, not tough skin. Rule #124.

Another key to promoting solidarity is being personally involved in every meeting or detail. Make sure not to appoint a "devil's advocate" for different meetings—that's the worst!

You can't have a person questioning your solutions. Allowing the group to look beyond your idea is insane! A jerk would never do that! Rule #13 forbids it (Dominate your conversations!), and Rule #15 backs it up (You're never not right.)!

A devil's advocate gives the group a chance to find alternate solutions.

It also could open up the avenue for other members to feel more comfortable bringing their ideas to light.

Don't set up standards for events or processes, and make sure that you as a leader don't fall into a standard people can grasp on to. If people can trust you'll act a certain way in any given situation they'll be more open to sharing their thoughts. Mix it up! If people can't follow along from meeting to meeting, they may keep quiet! That means less work for you!

On the flip side, we have the surefire pitfall. If you're trying to be a "goody-goody" (say it ain't so!). Don't do those things, unless there is another jerk trying to take over! Make sure you let others speak first on occasion, it will help the timid among your group feel more comfortable going against your ideas or perhaps even sharing better ones.

You can build relationships to battle against your foes! That's what relationships are all about, squashing your enemies! Squish, squish, squish!

Don't interrupt your peers. If you get into an argument and find yourself at a roadblock because they made a good point, you could explore that point instead of shutting it down or coming up with a counterpoint.

We'll pick up on how to argue like a jerk later on, but changing the topic and obfuscating the issue is very important for a jerk to master. You may be able to take hints from some public figures we all know!

Herd Mentality

Herd mentality, how else can you hope to manipulate and adjust life for everyone around you to better meet your own needs? I ask you!

This concept refers to how a herd of animals can be influenced to run away from a predator simply because they see others running without ever seeing what they are running from. This is also referenced as "mob mentality." It differs from groupthink, where you are perhaps be pressured to conform based on wanting to be liked, although it does relate closely.

Herd mentality discusses how a person can be influenced by a group to change their actions based on an emotional response, i.e. "tugging on your heartstrings", "running from the predator.", "the iPhone craze". It doesn't even require a set group or organization, but simply a gathering of people in a social venue.

Whereas groupthink deals more with a specific set of circumstances, conflict-avoidance, self-esteem, and normative influence (peer pressure) to maintain certain group harmonies, herd mentality is more emotionally influenced and not as guided.

I'll touch on technological sedatives a little later on. That topic is becoming more prevalent and evident as Silicon Valley is presented with evidence of influence beyond their control. I'm not so much talking about our lizard overlords influence from the flip side of the flat earth as much as economic algorithms within the systems of our social networks.

We can see the influences of herd mentality on an individual level in the things we buy. We see others buy the same items or the way our stock markets fluctuate from media coverage or certain people tweeting. Understanding herd mentality in this way leads us to the utilization of Jerk Rule #33 again, if people want to buy crap, it might as well be yours. Herd behavior factors into crowd psychology, which covers how crowds behave and how riots or sit-ins happen.

We won't go that deep and get into waves of influence and the like, but herd mentality plays a part in those responses as well.

A group of people can be influenced emotionally in multiple ways. Sadly, some groups understand that and use it to manipulate past the point of harm. That's a pretty A-Hole thing to do. Herd mentality also ebbs and flows, so it's a hard thing to control, as opposed to groupthink which has some structures that help produce or combat the process.

Herd mentality, however, is easy to spark, which makes it a dangerous thing. It's pretty easy to see. Sometimes herd mentality is exemplified when the media shares a news story that requires an emotional response and actionable follow-through. And sometimes its people coming together to do battle against children with cancer.... I mean support the fight against cancer in children. We're jerks, not monsters. We're not going to battle children with cancer!

Herd mentality can influence different groups and numbers of people. This mentality spreads based on the emotional impact of an inciting event. The number of people who witnessed it and their overall "power" in the world. The amount of time this mentality lasts in a society depends on the intensity of the shared reaction created by the witnesses.

You have seen the effects of herd mentality with this year's crisis. One group favors isolation, while another group seemingly wants to go back to work. Still, entire nations don't seem to have a concern one way or the other, and meanwhile, another group has made it a point to protest the crimes of police brutality amid these concerns.

More interesting to me than who is right or wrong on these topics is where the influence for each of these separate groups is coming from. Meanwhile, the media highlights both sides or, sometimes, whichever side it chooses to. Fascinating stuff, and it plays into the concept of power, which I'll touch on later.

Summary

We've talked on a high level about groups and organizations, how they influence us, and how groups can be used for good or bad. (Fraternities have had members die from hazing rituals while others have become leaders of the free world.)

I've touched on groupthink and how we can watch for it or enhance it within a group for maximum jerk influence. We also went over how herd mentality is a strong yet less-controllable social concept based on emotion rather than self-esteem. We can see the horrible effects of herd mentality more easily with our current social media sources and technology.

While these are interesting topics for jerks to dive deeper into, it's important to understand these concepts as we go about our day. We need to watch out for them in others as well as use them to our advantage. That's what a jerk does, after all; if we see an opportunity, we take it. Otherwise, some other jerk will.

Jerk Rules

So, what about these Jerk Rules that hold our world in place and out of global thermo-nuclear war?

Jerk Rule #13: Dominate the conversation - Negative Power potential.
    Pitfall: This takes a lot of effort. If you slack other people might be able to share their thoughts!

Jerk Rule #15: The number one rule: You're never not right.
    Pitfall: Don't forget this! It can lead to weakness! How could other people possibly be smarter than you?

Jerk Rule #29: People care about what you have to say.
    Pitfall: There is no pitfall here!

Jerk Rule #33: People like to buy crap, so why shouldn't they buy your crap?

BONUS Jerk Rule #40: Don't worry about completing every little thing, that's what others are for. Half-assing is okay in the information age, one might say it's even expected or encouraged.
    Pitfall: Letting other people help you out can cause them to like you! You've been warned!

Jerk Rule #47: Be friends with people who will hold you back. Sometimes it's easier to be a jerk if you have nothing going for you. If you have deadbeat friends, they can help with that!
    Pitfall: Sometimes you can be held back too much and sink into not being useful at all.

Jerk Rule #87: If you don't work the system, the system won't work.
    Pitfall: In working the system sometimes you form relationships. Be careful about these, they might lead to healthy group dynamics!

Jerk Rule #141: Generalizing for the sake of an argument. Who cares about getting to the truth? Use all the fallacies you can to win. (Discussed later, what do you want from me! Order? We're about chaos baby! At least a little from time to time, not too much.)

You ever wonder why all the people around you are lazy, irresponsible, angry, and out to get you? Me too. It probably has something to do with our next topic of being a jerk. Projecting. The ego's shield. Don't want to deal with it? Project it!

How can we use this protective, yet corrosive aspect of ourselves that makes us jerky and distant to our benefit you ask? Glad you asked, I'll walk you through it!

CHAPTER 5
PROJECTING
PROJECTING GOALS VS. SHORTCOMINGS

"Don't be a reflection of your depression, your dark, or your ugly. Reflect what you want. Your light, your beauty, and your strength. Aspire for greatness – reflect who you are; not which deficits you maintain. Showcase the hidden treasures."

—

Tiffany Luard

Projecting. Think of it as your ego's shield. Tiffany sounds like a "goodie-two-shoes."

You may have heard of this concept. In a nutshell, projecting can be thought of as a defensive function of the ego. We'll get into that beast a little later in the book.

I want to cover three areas on this topic to help you understand the path you need to walk to become the jerk you'd like to be. If we don't understand ourselves, we can't hope to properly utilize our full jerk potential. We'll be too busy watching all the massively impressive entertainment, reading up on the latest news, and sinking into a warm blanket of comfort!

Comfort breeds gooeyness and that's what spiders feeds off of! That's the quote, right? Maybe it was complacency. Anyway, it's a problem when you're stuck behind your shield. You're always looking out at the obstacles in front of you, and not the ones behind (within) you.

The first area to think about deals with Carl Jung's concept known as "the shadow" and how we can create projections of those aspects of ourselves onto others. In going over this information, you'll glean at least on a surface-level the knowledge of what makes us tick in this area. With it perhaps you can analyze your actions in a new light.

Not that goody-goody "light" Tiffany was talking about, but like the light focused through a magnifying glass to burn ants with kinda "light".

The second area in projection deals with projective identification, as in how people "push" an idea onto someone else. This concept has many functions, and not all are as negative as how Chancellor Palpatine manipulated Anakin in that War among the Stars so long ago.

Like many things in our world, projective identification can be used for good and bad. I want to discuss both in three parts. First, how parents find themselves using it, probably for the good; second, how we can use it to become empathic and enhance our intuitive skills; and third, how it relates to a term called "gaslighting."

The final big area we should talk about is projecting in terms of goals. It's a completely different topic than the ones I've already mentioned, but it has a huge impact on our self-image and ties into our goal setting. It deals with how we form, look at, and accomplish our goals, and it has a great deal to do with how we perceive ourselves in viewing those goals.

This overarching concept of goal projection has a cascading effect that can influence how we see ourselves and what we project onto others, both positive and negative. This is by far the most important topic of the chapter to understand and properly apply, but it builds on the previous topics.

Classic Projection – The Work of the Shadow – Area 1

"Who knows what evil lurks in the hearts of men? The Shadow knows..." Or at least that's what the intro to the 1930s radio broadcast of the infamous detective serial used to say.

The shadow we're talking about here, though, is a concept of Jungian design. It deals with the side of ourselves that is perhaps not entirely conscious but has influence over aspects of our understandings.

This "dark half," if you're comfortable splitting yourself up in such a rudimentary way, is mainly thought to house negative attributes of character. That is a limited understanding of the shadow. This part of our psyche can also hold back the more positive attributes we possess but don't give ourselves the credit for having. The shadow hides. The shadow lies. It also contains and tries to feed our negatives for the sake of comfort. Comfort breeds entropy.

In the simplest terms, you can think of the shadow as a source of concrete thought but it isn't solely purposeful as one might think of something that has true motivation. Inside the mind, it acts as a chaotic incubator of waste and generates thoughts such as, "I'm not good enough." "Let's wait till tomorrow." "It's too complex." "Let's go for it!" "I want that!"

The shadow is more than just a holding place; it also works silently, unconsciously, reaching out to nourish these negative thoughts, all for the sake of homeostasis or pleasure. It's more than Freud's id and instinct, and less watched over as well.

If you're a helpful person, you might find you can't say, "no." Or if you're kind, "telling your truth" might not be something you're comfortable expressing. These also have a place in the thing Jung calls the shadow.

The shadow attacks purposeful intentions without us being aware. It impedes progress by dangling comfort or presenting impossibility at the task at hand.

However, we don't tend to notice the work of our shadows, but rather we see ample room for growth in other people's actions or lack thereof. Our ego projecting.

If we don't confront our shadow head-on, that negative aspect will grow inside us. The shadow whispers to the ego. I don't always stick to a schedule, but I do acknowledge that I need to. Without acknowledging my procrastination I might find that I project it onto others causing agitation with them. Even though they may not actually be procrastinating. How can I know what they are thinking? Jerks know! Rule #163! More on that later.

That's a good indicator of psychological projection, which acts as a defense mechanism so we don't have to confront our own limitations. When we can explain the reason for someone's actions (or inaction) and that reason drives the emotion in me, that's a good example of projection.

We can't know what people are thinking, or in certain instances what they're going through. No matter how awesome we think we are. I know we as jerks like to think we do. While I would encourage mind reading, it is producing a limitation in reaching your full jerk potential.

Here's an example: When I see someone being outwardly vocal in a meeting, I cringe. Why? Maybe it's because I think they're selfish or rude. Maybe I don't like conflict. It could be one of those, or maybe it's because I see that they speak their mind, and I *don't* do that.

Speaking my mind is buried in my shadow because I'm afraid of what others think of me. I don't want to sound stupid or upsetting. I tend to fall into the more agreeable side of the agreeable/aggressive scale, which lends itself to this sort of attitude. When you fear others, you do yourself a disservice.

Jerks shouldn't care, but at the same time isolation helps you be a better jerk! If you only listen to yourself, you're always going to be right!

But the cringe I get exemplifies how classic projection works. It's not something we do all the time, mind you; maybe that person who spoke up in the meeting is just a jerk, but the projection is something to watch for. If we know to watch for it, we can confront it and "grow".

Another example of projection could be when we're having a conversation with someone close to us, and they ask an "oh so innocent question":

"Did you get your home/yard/project work done that you wanted to?"

Now, if you spent all day getting ready for your middle-weight prizefight with a grizzly bear match coming up in late November or spent it virtually beating up chickens with a sword instead of doing actual work you might have a thought to snap at them. Why, though? All they're doing is asking a question.

Asking the question was the action on their part. Simply because you feel judged by the question does not mean it was presented in a judging manner. Your assumption is the perceived reason, and that reason is why you became upset. That's a form of projecting.

People do this all the time on social media. It's easy to misinterpret the intention of the text. Perhaps you feel guilty because you knew you were supposed to do your homework, clean the yard, or write the next chapter of your book.

Maybe it's a good idea not to snap at a person who is simply engaging with you, to develop that relationship instead of burning it down... but of course, we're learning how to be jerks here so, we don't need no water. So, if that's you, keep it up! You're doing great.

Why do we do this? Why do we constantly think we know others' true intentions in every situation? Because we are projecting what we feel about ourselves onto someone else's questions. They might not even have thought about it being a question that could provoke us to be defensive. Most likely, they just wanted to engage with you.

Or maybe they're trolls. I hate trolls, but you can't always know they're trolling.

It might seem like this always happens to you. Everyone is judging us. Then, after we release our venom-filled answer on them we create more distance in our relationships.

So, what do you do to nurture your networks and expand your jerk potential beyond the walls of your parent's basement? You become an analyst. When you're talking or before you talk with someone, ask yourself these simple questions:

- What's the actual core subject of conversation, outside the words? What's the goal?
- How do I feel about it?
- Am I connected to the topic at hand?
- Is my ego attached to this topic, and if so, why?
- What needs to be done in the conversation? What's the end goal?
- Am I doing my part to promote truth, or just protecting my ego?

These questions shouldn't take more than five seconds for you to gauge. Although in the beginning, you may have to give them more time or ask them directly to the person you are engaging with. Nothing wrong with that—it opens up communication. Although that could be strange and you may sound like Sheldon from the *Big Bang Theory*.

I know this doesn't sound jerky, but you need to maximize your potential and life isn't just black and white... until it is.

When you talk with other people, listen to them, and ask yourself follow-up questions:

- What are their words?
- What does their body language say?
- In past interactions, how have I felt about this person?
- Did they say something that upset me? If so why?
- Did they mean to upset me, or did they simply do something and I took offense?
- Did they ask me something that I felt bad about, but they didn't know it?

These questions can help you determine if you might be projecting. Sometimes we have conversations and people say things that offend us. If we look at where that other person is coming from, we may be able to use our analysis to determine they didn't mean anything by it.

If someone's actions upset us, yet they don't seem to notice, this might be a time to reflect on the event. It might be that we are simply projecting something onto them because of our assumptions or because our ego secretly views the event that way.

If you're a "happy-go-lucky" person, don't worry so much. Remember when I said to tread lightly? Over-analyzation leads to paralyzation. Enjoy people and conversations. This tool of cool (headiness) should give freedom, not be used as a cage. Don't turn it into one.

Projective Identification – Area 2

Projective Identification is an interesting thing. This is how some people "push" an idea onto someone else. There are multiple applications of this term.

Projective identification doesn't have to be all bad, although that means taking an active role in understanding its influence. For parents who take their kids to soccer practice or a Cobra Kai dojo, there is a certain level of expectation. Remember what projecting is though: it's taking something from within ourselves and attributing it to something remote.

When it comes to children, parents already feel. (*Some* parents, I should say. Some parents are too self-involved to have an actual connection, tragically.) This existing connection makes it easy for us to push ourselves onto our children.

Some of our expectations for others come from an expectation of ourselves. While the understanding of expectations is another field of psychology, it's related to projection in general and is directed outwardly in projective identification.

If I were a black belt in Cobra Kai, I might feel that my imaginary daughter should be too. I might be hard on her, to push her forward, which might not work. It could be a negative force that makes her feel worse. Perhaps making her give up entirely under the pressure.

If she failed to perform a kata, I might be disappointed because I'd be projecting on her the first kata that I passed. A passionate yet disappointed parent at a sporting event is a great example of negative projective identification.

Instead of using this connection we have with our children in such a negative way, we could step back and look at different ways to engage. We are not our children; we do not get to live vicariously through them. Our children have their own lives. We as a society, as a village, are responsible for helping them succeed. They watch us always. They will emulate you.

Whenever I didn't do something well as a kid, I was disappointed enough. Although not all children feel such a burden of responsibility. Everyone can't be as cool as I am!

Projective identification has a negative connotation to it, but it doesn't have to. I can positively identify with someone and then project those positive aspects on to that person. This is a tool that can help build or break down self-esteem in others. Even if they're not real aspects of character that person has. Our perception is our reality.

This positivity could lead to unchecked praise, which as you know is a path of the jerk. Sometimes our feelings or lives get overloaded and we don't see what we project onto others. Just as others don't see what we project in our minds. Great... another spot to analyze ourselves.

What's one way to ensure our projective identification is working positively for people and not affecting them or us negatively? Well, honestly, I have no guarantees, but I do have an exercise to help limit those negative projections onto others.

Recall that jerks aren't out to harm others. Being supportive to build others up only helps your "power" as a jerk! When you win, you win! It's really all about you!

There are two aspects to this. First, you need to feel good about yourself. You shouldn't lie about how you feel to others and put on a front to make others feel good, but nor should you project your negative outlook on them either.

This means focused vocalization. You could speak about your concerns or negative feelings to someone who can help but don't bare your soul to just anyone who comes down the street. Don't lay that burden on your children, either. You should find support, whether in a group or in meeting with a professional.

The second aspect is, as you are seeking help, be helpful to others. Be kind, friendly, and positive, even when you're not feeling positive. As made popular by Ellen and echoed by me, "Be kind to yourself and one another." It's easy to say, but life makes us forget ourselves sometimes.

You have to focus on the good things about yourself, and you have to encourage yourself in gray and dark times. One way to do this, besides seeking a support structure or professional help, is capturing your thoughts.

Although you should be careful in using these tactics, they could lead to being a "goody-two-shoes" if you're not careful! Always fall back on the rules to avoid the pitfalls!

Back to this idea of positive projection though—if we could support our children by not projecting our negative aspects and thoughts but rather our potential (checked praise) onto them, we would go a long way in helping their self-esteem.

Just because you're training to be a jerk doesn't mean you don't care about others; it just means you shouldn't have to care as much! Remember in building others up, this gives you more "power"!

All that said, sometimes we have to push ourselves and our children to perform, which leads to testing and exceeding our perceived limits as presented by our shadows. My fictionally projected daughter still needs to master the crane kick to take out Johnny Lawrence and make it to the top of the Dojo!

Empathy and Intuition – Who Needs it? Well… Jerks Do.

We've looked at how connections and projective identification can affect children and create in them either positive or negative attributes for their self-esteem. Now let's talk about how projective identification can enrich our empathy and intuitive skills.

To explain the connections, we'll use the friendship dynamic this time. Let's bring in peer pressure as well for good measure.

It's important to understand the dynamics of a relationship if you want to be a really big jerk. If you only want to be an average run-of-the-mill jerk, it's less important. You can get it wrong without reading this all on your own, but I'm here to guide you!

Your best friend is called your "best" friend for a reason. You know the kind I'm talking about: a friend who will let you know when you shouldn't drink till you pass out or who tells you when you're being a bully to improve your character. A *real* best friend. Not one that helps you bury bodies. One that stops you from needing to.

You'll find yourself spending tons of time with them. That's one thing I loved about being a teenager. I had a lot of time to spend with my friends—the good ones and the bad.

As you spend time with someone, you find yourself doing different things, like going to the mall, amusement parks, and on road trips. That's a lot of time for talking (or for spending time on your phone, but that's more in line with jerk rule #68) and getting to know each other.

You talk about boys and girls, sports and games. You become familiar with what's going on in your friend's lives and not getting just a snapshot of what's happening from a virtual wall of constant updates directed by an algorithm concerned with generating the most money. Interactions like these give us a real human connection.

These human connections also help us to "read" each other. If we don't make time for these human connections, we'll have a harder time developing "soft skills" that the professional world hopes you have.

Don't worry—if you're smart, you get a pass. Our economy likes smart people. After all, the smarter you are, the harder you'll work! I feel like that has to be a slogan out of the novel *1984*, or at least on some posters in the city of Rapture from the videogame *Bioshock*.

While we make these connections, we bring with us our personalities, the good and the bad. No way around it. That's good, though, because to grow, we need these messy connections.

One thing that might happen is projective identification; with our friends, sometimes we test each other. "Do they like what I like?" You might mention a topic to feel out their knowledge on something.

If you think your friends are cool, chances are you might feel cool around them. If your friends are smart, you might feel smart. More importantly, you might start looking into new topics, like science and math, sports, history, games, or technology.

You might find yourself projecting your values or the values of your friends. These interactions can and do lead to a tool called mirroring.

Mirroring is an unconscious mental utility that can help create a connection between people. Projective identification pushes our thoughts and our values onto others, or it helps us relate and take up others' thoughts and values. Mirroring is commonly explained as the way a person may copy someone else's mannerisms in a conversation.

We'll discuss more on mirroring in a section on body language. All these things are connected together! I want you to understand these concepts to maximize your jerk potential!

Projective identification helps build affective empathy (shared feelings) as well as mirroring the values of that person. On the negative side of this coin is peer pressure. We might mirror actions to be seen as part of a group.

Growing up the natural use of projective identification enhances our affective empathy. It also bolsters our ability to feel what the people around us feel. Building on that, these interactions help us build what is called cognitive empathy. This type of empathy allows us to understand what another person is feeling.

As we gain empathic knowledge we can enhance our intuitive skills. The more we learn about other people, the more tools we have to analyze our own feelings and thoughts with a more well-rounded set of skills.

Gaslighting

> *"I hear noises and footsteps. I imagine things, that there are people over the house. I'm frightened, and of myself too."* – Paula Alquist Anton, *Gaslight*, 1944

I've never seen this old movie, but it sounds utterly terrifying. I'll quickly summarize it. This terrible man named George married a woman named Paula, who is well-off… so well-off that she has jewels stashed in her attic.

George is a grifter, a conman, and he wants those jewels for himself. The attic jewels aren't in plain sight. George has to find them and he has to do it on the down-low, without revealing his intentions to Paula.

He also needs to get away after he finds them. So he comes up with the idea to tell her things that didn't happen, you know lying. This isn't just lying though; this is an attempt to push a new reality onto Paula. He's lying to make her think she's going mad.

To do so, he changes things around the house. In the morning, when Paula makes note of it, George explains various things. "You moved that picture. Don't you remember?" Paula references the gaslights are dimmer in the room and George denies this even though he turned them down and so he could turn the ones up in the attic to search for the jewels.

These lies and others help cover the noises of him bumping around in the attic at night, hunting for the jewels. The play/movie gets its name from the gaslights he dims in the house.

This is a form of subtle psychological manipulation where the manipulator works to make a victim distrust their thoughts or beliefs. If you find yourself doing this to someone, I encourage you to seek help. I know this book teaches how to be a jerk, but this isn't a jerk move—this is an asshole move. Remember that line from the definition I gave upfront? Yea, this counts as intentional harm.

If you're a victim or an abuser who wants to stop the chaotic cycle in your life, reach out. The Greatist.com website has a list of twenty-two organizations that support victims of domestic abuse. There are national and international organizations on the list.

I'd also point out the World Health Organization has a listing of international organizations that can help in this regard. These references are in the appendix, but you can just as quickly search for them on the Internet.

The more you know about a tool in an abuser's toolbox, the better you can defend against them.

On a darker level, this isn't simply a tactic used in relationships; there are incidents of gaslighting in the office, between politicians, and even references to how the media and even our technology has used this. Where are my conspiracy readers at?! I wonder if the Mandela Effect is just one big gaslighting experiment.

Again, I think it's important to point this out on a personal level, because if you don't know it's happening, how can you point it out?

Anyway, onto more positive jerk things!

Projecting Goals – Area 3

We all have to maintain our everyday lives. We have work and family. Throw in everyday errands and tasks, most of which are easy to manage and it can be hard to reach those personal goals.

Do we have time for such a thing as personal goals with everything else we have to worry about nowadays? It certainly doesn't feel like it. How do projecting goals help make me a better jerk, you ask?

Well, if you're like me and set goals and then have a hard time following through with them, it can affect your overall attitude toward the people in your life, at work, and home. The way we look at goals, how we form them in our minds, and how we accomplish these milestones has a great deal to do with how we come to perceive ourselves.

This overarching concept has a cascading effect that can influence how we treat ourselves and what we project onto others, either by feeding our "shadow" or promoting worth within ourselves and our ability to promote it within those around us.

Let's take lifestyle goals. We'll start with an easy one: working out.

What's the goal? You want to look good. That was my goal too; I mean, as a closet narcissist, I already look good, but better never hurts!

When I start working out, I normally have a vague plan that starts with me wanting to look like the people on that workout commercial. That's never going to happen, by the way. I don't have it in me; I want to write more than I want to work out.

When coming up with a plan for my goal, I say to myself, "I'm going to do these exercises, on these days, for this amount of time, and I'm going to get these results!". Do I write it down? No, who wants to have a reminder?

And then at the end of the month, I weigh myself and look in the mirror. I've lost three pounds. That wasn't the result I was looking for, despite all that time working out. I also didn't see much change in the mirror, if any. So much for that goal! The result was not what I wanted, so the goal remains out of reach, as well as vague because I only have the goal in my head. No written plan. So far to go, yet not close enough to continue.

Let's take another goal for example writing. I want to write a book.

Okay, let's make a plan. I'm going to come up with an outline and set aside a few days a week to write after my day job. At the end of the month, I'll have an outline and four chapters done. That sounds like a good plan and goal!

The end of the month rolls around, and I look over my writing plan. It turns out it took a little longer to research those topics, and I got a little sidetracked by some family things. No worries—I'll do the same thing next month and get *six* chapters done instead.

By the end of the second month, I have four chapters done, and in reading them over, I realize I'm going to need to rewrite. (Note: It always seems like I have to rewrite but that's an instance where my shadow is talking to me.)

On top of that utter failure, I wanted to have six chapters done, not just four! How am I ever going to do this with so many distractions? The result is not what I wanted, so the goal remains out of reach.

This happens to us when setting goals because we are taking what is called a "results-oriented approach.". Of course, the goal of looking better is a result, and the result of writing a book is having written a book, but those are the end goals. It's where we want to be, not where we are.

What happens is we trip up on the intermediate results. If my goal is to lose weight and look better, but during my planning, I place a milestone marker saying I need to lose three pounds by this specific point, I could be setting myself up for failure. It's great to have markers like this and write them down but this shouldn't be a determining factor in continuing to reach a bigger end goal.

If I determine that I have to write four chapters a month to finish my book, I could be setting myself up for failure. (That might be a really low bar or a high one depending on who you are and where you're at in life.)

Have you ever heard the saying, "it's about the journey, not the destination?" That's true for a goal as well. When we set up these expectations, we're creating checkpoints in our minds. "If I don't get this result by this time, it's not going to happen," or at least that's what we're allowing ourselves to say in the back of our heads.

Maybe this works for work projects with multiple people pushing you along, but it can be a showstopper when we apply them at home. Perhaps we should view our goal creation differently.

Now, this is going to sound strange, but don't set a result. I'm talking crazy, right? After all, how can you hope to measure your progress without a result? You do it by comparing yourself to the version of yourself from last week.

If I'm writing, I know I feel good about myself. I don't know why. Maybe I like feeling productive, even if I'm not selling or publishing at that moment.

If I'm working out, how do I feel? Probably tired! Working out is hard, and I don't see any results in the mirror, but I'm working out. My real goal was to feel better about how I look. I see the beautiful people on TV and feel bad about myself, but even though I look the same in the mirror last week as I do this week, I am working toward eliminating that feeling and that's good!

That approach is far better than saying to myself, "I'm just a huge sack of couch potato!" The realization or effort of working out should make you feel good about continuing to work out because it is not about the destination—it's about the journey.

When I want to set a goal, nine times out of ten it is something that I want to get done, and not getting it done means that either I will feel worse for not doing it, or I'll lose interest in the goal because I hit a wall.

I'll tell myself it doesn't matter, and I'll quit. Then, eventually, someone will ask an innocent question I'll project on to, or maybe an ad on TV will make me uncomfortable for not doing it, and the cycle begins again.

Let's step back. I want to achieve all of my goals either because of outside influences or a desire for personal growth.

If it's an outside influence, like an office project or doing the dishes for the family, these small and large goals have enough structure around them that I don't have to explain how to manage them.

If it's losing weight, ask yourself why. Is it because you saw someone on a commercial and they looked better, or perhaps you are having a hard time meeting someone, or you simply want to feel better about yourself? Okay, so that could fall into outside or internal influence or both at the same time.

In this "information age," existing systems enable us to more easily compare ourselves to others, as I've mentioned. Have you ever met someone and the first question one of you asked each other was, "So, what do you do for work?"

I get that it's a way to connect, but it's also a way to compare. Do they do something more or less important than I do? Probably less, I mean I'm freaking awesome. I'm sure you are too! Jerks are awesome!

Television and Hollywood, magazines, YouTube, marketing and sports, the downward spiral of human nature. All these things have helped us to compare ourselves to others.

My outlook is different. If I compare myself to you and what you have, I would never measure up. If I compare myself to Bill Gates... well, Bill Gates and I are pretty tight, but let's just say that if I compared myself to his lifestyle, I couldn't measure up. Or let's take it down a notch to a semi-unknown yet successful author, say Drew Karpyshyn. I fall short of Drew every time too.

More accurately I'm lining myself up to a moving target. If I find someone whom I feel is just a little "lesser" than me, I might feel better about myself, but that doesn't require any effort on my part to become better. Even my brothers, who are in my mind "equal" to me—I couldn't compete with them. The only person I can compare myself to is me.

When I do this, I can properly grade my results (that's the thing I warned you about previously) against how I did yesterday. And let me tell you, if I don't measure up when I'm looking at my past self, I wield all the power to adjust my outlook and my goals for today. We can set a goal, and if we're getting closer to it by any amount, we're succeeding.

There is also an aspect of not lying to yourself about goals. If I continue to watch attractive people on TV and feel bad about not working out or writing a bestseller, yet I don't do anything to mitigate that feeling, perhaps I don't truly care. And if I don't truly care, maybe I shouldn't beat myself up in the mirror about it and move forward in my life.

Oh, that thing about my brothers being equal, yeah... that's not true at all. They're way better than me! I'm a professional jerk!

Summary

Projection is powerful.

In its negative forms, the "shadow" allows us to lash out at people who may not have meant to hurt us at all. If those feelings are negative, that's a golden opportunity to be jerks about it, even if the other person didn't mean it the way we thought.

Another outward-facing form of projection is more often used for "pushing" ideas onto others. Sometimes we can use this method to push a more positive outlook to those around us if we're intentional about it. Jerk's need networks too!

Not to say we should hide our negative feelings. If you are having trouble with depression please reach out to someone close or to an organization that can help. After all, a depressed jerk may be jerkier but usually not as effective toward their goals.

The final topic of Projection Identification can also help us increase our empathic abilities and enhance our intuitive skills as we grow and interact with others. This doesn't apply to projection between a therapist and a patient as some level of trust is needed for that healing bond.

Projective Identification also reaches beyond jerkdom. If you find yourself thinking of how to cause doubt in someone, it's safe to say you're approaching that line between jerk and A-hole. Gaslighting doesn't simply stop at personal relationships; gaslighting can happen to anyone, anywhere—in the workspace, in politics, the media, and within our technological hive mind.

The last topic I covered was projecting goals. We tend to start off projecting goals that we either give up on halfway through, or we'll complete them but feel like it wasn't what we wanted. To create obtainable goals, write them up, and stop going for results. We should just enjoy the ride. Also, a bonus tip, view yourself reaching the goal. Visualize and make a plan.

Some of this comes from how we compare ourselves. In our world, we can easily compare ourselves to others—what they have, what we don't have, etc.

When we do this, it's hard, if not impossible, to measure up. Shooting a moving target always is. Duck Hunt was impossible! But if we flip our view to comparing ourselves from where we're at, to where we've been, the idea of goal-setting or even gaining results becomes altogether different.

Maybe try it out. Unless you just want to sit there and listen to your shadow.

Jerk Rules

Jerk Rule #68: When you're doing something with friends, it's always important to check your phone to make sure your friends that aren't there are aware of what you're doing. This will also serve to help alienate the friends you're actually with, which is ideal. This ties into rule #75 on dating as well.

Pitfall: Technology will help you with this. Don't turn off your notifications. Listen for that ding. Bored? Jump on the Internet instead of going for a walk with a friend! #HypnoToad

BONUS Jerk Rule #127: Other people don't know what they're doing. You should expect you have to guide them.

Okay, we've talked about aspects of what make us do jerky things but why are we jerks? What's the core that drives us. Maybe it's things we picked up from our parents, and maybe it's got to do with projecting. But I think it has more to do with this next topic.

It's misunderstood, it's not who we are, but it is nonetheless lurking inside of us like a spider waiting to inject venom in those around us while turning our insides into a soft gooey mess at the same time. If we're soft inside we won't have the strength to be the best jerks we can be.

Well, I say it's time we start fighting back. To do that let's take a look at how we can view the massive concept we call ego.

CHAPTER 6
EGO

WHAT IS EGO? WHAT IS PRIDE? HOW TO MANAGE THESE IN THE TIME WHERE EVERYTHING MATTERS.

"Receive without pride, let go without attachment."

—

Marcus Aurelius

I love talking about deep things. It makes me feel so much smarter than other people! I find that discussing technology and potential societal and economic impacts is both highly interesting and entertaining. And it makes me better (though it's hard to improve on perfection). I'm getting my truth out there!

However, I believe even us jerks should be aware of a real truth. Simply discussing topics with no real follow-up action is an utter waste of time. You need clear direction.

Remember that everyone has a motive. Trolls are formed on this earth to fill it with noise. Noise is one of our enemies.

In light of that, I find that understanding various topics and having conversations has helped me navigate my interactions with others. It helps correct my thinking, as well as understanding where others might be coming from, which increases my cognitive empathy skills.

Of course, all of this "growth" is to benefit myself. Don't forget that.

In order to gain support for your causes, you may need to correct your thinking and manage your emotions. To do that, we need to discuss some tools. With these tools, we can decrease the noise of all the other jerks out there. This noise doesn't always come from the trolls in the world but also from within ourselves as we've previously discussed. Your shadow produces noise.

First, I want to go over some definitions of what we're talking about, especially since I'm blending psychological schools of thought regarding the ego and the shadow concerning Carl Jung and Dr. Freud's works on the subject.

The id/ego/superego are three main aspects of the psyche that Sigmund Freud defined to describe a person's thoughts and drives by assigning labels to them. In this chapter, we're only interested in the ego.

Previously I spoke about the "shadow" that Jung wrote about. The concept of the shadow could be correlated to the id, but unlike the id, the shadow reaches over into the superego as it influences ego. All I'm saying is, it's not a one-to-one comparison.

Jung's shadow contains more than just our hidden primal desires and instinctual drives. The shadow could be seen as a defense mechanism, unlike projection which is utilized by the ego as an outward shield against others.

The shadow manipulates the superego's "shame finger" or "rule setter" to meet the will of its chaotic nature, and it creates noise within our mind that can make it hard to focus on what truly matters to us. But enough about the shadow for now. We've got egotistical fish to fry.

As jerks, we should always go to the source of something to learn truth. Secondhand knowledge is at best like being the third person in a game of telephone. It's probably right, but we have to trust the person telling us the info more than we probably should.

If we're always just making crap up, it's harder to get people to believe us!

And as jerks, we should recall how that old 90's television show *The X-Files* laid out one of the great Jerk Rule to guide us: Rule #14 – Trust no one. Also, Aliens are behind everything.

I always like to verify, and then I trust. Before I hired my editor, I checked him out. Made sure he knew what he's doing, that he'd done this sort of project before, and that he hadn't edited any flat earth books. It's important to verify, especially in this age where anyone can be an "influencer", but that should be common sense in any era of mankind. It's one of my more "jerk-like" qualities, I just don't trust you. Real jerks say they verify and have legit sources, but a lot of people don't. That's because they take just enough of something and spin it for their cause.

Learn well grasshopper. Seek truth for your purposes, not for the sake of truth alone.

Now, jerks shouldn't believe anything without verifying it first, but it's hard to keep up with all the lies. They spread so fast in our hyperconnected society. This brings us to Rule #123 – As a jerk, you can believe anything you want, just make sure there is a grain of truth to twist first.

It's good to verify facts, and this helps when you're in a heated argument on politics or religion, or how toilet paper should be properly dispensed. As a jerk, you already know the right answer to this, so I don't have to explain to you that real jerks don't even use toilet paper. Jerk Rule #315. Jerks smell like roses anyway.

Note this addendum to Jerk Rule #123: Whereas jerks can believe anything we want, when dealing with others, we should only believe what can be verified based on our standards. Jerks don't need to verify what they say, but rather only sound like they have.

Even still, sometimes our feelings blind us to presenting our truth, so why is that. Let's explore this. What is Ego? Let's ask the man himself.

Freud says in his paper *The Ego and the Id*, (Freud, 1923): "*The functional importance of the ego is manifested in the fact that normally control over the approaches to motility devolves upon it.*"

Then he goes into describing a man on a horse with the instinctual id being the horse and the ego being the man. I have to thank Dr. Siggy for being oh-so crystal clear on the functional aspects here, but perhaps he was using rule #167 which reminds us jerks to use abstraction so the layman will be able to add on their understanding while insisting that the source knew what they were talking about and justifying their own jerk interpretations. #JerksOfTheWorldUnite

What I derive from his example is that the ego is the aspect that helps us control, administer, or harness our "wild Hyde side."

By contrast, our superego would be likened to the riding instructor who knows all the rules for riding that horse (id) and the rules that should be followed. If not, the superego yells at us for not doing it right, and if we're not serial killers, then we might feel shame about it.

That description sounds simple enough, but here's another so you won't try to stab me: The ego is the aspect of ourselves that balances desire and morals and links to things we care about. Sigmund also described the ego as a sense of self but later adjusted it to better explain its functionality.

I am going to stick with the definition that the ego is how we organize ourselves, not who we are. According to Freud, the ego is not who we are—it's *less* than who we are. It's only one aspect. It's how we maintain ourselves mentally.

I wanted to point that out as there is another topic about the ego, you'll see floating around the Internets. It's called "ego death" in spiritual circles, otherwise known as "psychic death" by Carl Jung. I believe the honorary jerk Timothy Leary called it "ego loss."

I'm not trying to discredit these notions; I don't think I have to. (Yes, I'm that arrogant. And handsome, too.) The concept of "ego death" doesn't take the definition of ego as Freud presents it seriously, so I don't want it getting in the way of what I'm going to talk about.

As I mentioned, the ego is only one aspect within us. All three of these aspects (ego, id, superego) and their interactions make up who we are... for the most part. That is what I want to stick to. Ego death tends to mesh these concepts, and thinking on or drawing from this "death of self" idea will simply add confusion to my points.

While ego death can create valid discussions, I don't see its applicability in teaching you how to be a better jerk. I'm all for enlightenment, but I want to talk about how to become the best jerk you can be. Enlightenment carries a certain weight and vibe with it that turns some people off. I'm not talking about hocus pocus. I want you to have useful tools.

After all, we at the School Stoppers aren't trying to make you better people; we're trying to make you better jerks!

If we consider the ego to be an administrator of the desire of the id and the morals provided by the superego, it gives us a foundation to work from. It's the aspect that labels, organizes knowledge, and compares. We can see how it's hard for an educated person, a.k.a. someone that's read my book, not to connect your whole self to that aspect. That's what people do, right? We compare and label. The ego does this, ergo we are ego. That's wrong.

I don't think we should take the ego to be ourselves. I've said the ego is only a part of the whole—the whole being the id, ego, superego, shadow, the didgeridoo, and the unidentified twenty-one grams from the famous 1907, twenty-one grams experiment. (Don't bother looking into those last two; the second is a reference to the soul, and the other is an Australian wind instrument.).

Needless to say, the ego is not, and should never be considered alone, the determining factor of who you are.

Instead of the rider on the horse, let's make the ego something easy to grasp. I hope no one is afraid of spiders, because I want you to picture a web and this web is huge, like if Shelob from *Lord of the Rings* had one.

The web strands reach out and connect to different experiences from your whole life—how your friends treat you, the stuff you know about geek trivia or sports statistics, what your beliefs are.

Another ten web strands reach out to how you look or what you weigh. Others reach out to your superego or what you believe is right. Another one reaches over to your experiences in having a family, buying and owning a home, or car. We've also got threads created from bad information. How the world works, how someone else should be, it goes on and on.

Imagine that the web is covered in light and shadow. Some strings are easy to see, and some are hidden in the darkness of the grey. Now, remember the web and the spider aren't you. Thank God, right? We love our stance on what we think and know. It took time to build the web, and frankly, if you're being honest, it looks kinda cozy and organized. Just how you like it.

Nice and complacent—everything a growing jerk needs.

You can pull on a string and bring up your knowledge on the strange experiment from 1907 to impress your readers or yank on another to think about how you feel about your friends and what they mean to you. Our ego spider makes these webs and strings all the time, whether from learning new things to forming a new relationship at work. It protects it to, with emotion.

I like my web. It holds things together. Sometimes, though, a person comes along and pulls at some of those strings, even ripping them away.

This is when things get messy. Spiders don't like it when you pull on their web! We get hurt and as you might expect from an arachnid, it steadies itself for an attack. Your spider works on instinct. It wants to protect the web it's helped make, and dying isn't an option. So how can we view these interactions that tug on our threads?

Your web was hard to make. It took time. There's pride involved in that. Someone might come along with comments on what you're eating, and subsequently, you two engage in an argument. Maybe they simply made a comment that felt cold.

Like I told you, I bust my friend's chops from time to time, but words can no doubt hurt. Keep in mind Jerk Rule #125: You need thick skin to be a jerk!

In an argument, this person might have better points than you because they've done actual research and you didn't. See the pitfall in not verifying things before you say them? Perhaps they won't even listen to your side of things and instead bully you with argumentative fallacies.

In those trying times, web strands can be damaged or even broken, and you might want to lash out in an effort to protect them. Your spider would expect it! What's important to remember is that we are *not* the web, nor are we the spider.

What happens in these events is that we come away from them *thinking* we've been hurt. I'm not trying to downplay those events or associated emotions. I can't know your tragedy or emotional state. However, as a jerk in training, you might benefit from looking at these events differently.

Of course, these arguments and accusations hurt us because we're attached to these ideas. These events shape my life and me. They are my world because perception is reality.

These strands hold our understandings of the world together, and when one or more get broken, we've been wronged! Your spider rears up in attack mode and whispers in that creepy spidery voice, "Weee should break sssome of theiiirrr striiinnngggsss?!"

But remember, these webs are *not* you. They're concepts and ideas and events you're attached to, for sure, but they are not you. Maybe there is an idea with a string you're connected to because it's right. So you protect that string at the expense of others, and different strings get broken. Maybe the wrong string. Maybe it's a relationship. That happens a lot in life.

I'm not saying that getting your strands broken is in any way easy, but perhaps we can better manage the fallout when they do get broken. Instead of the spider trying to defend or attack, perhaps it could sit still. Real spiders don't lunge out immediately after a web is broken. They look at *why* the strand broke. They build different ones.

Let's ask ourselves, what, exactly, was it connected to? If you can't point it out, you'll need to learn this introspection to adapt and grow. If you want to be a jerk, you gotta play the game. If you can't take the heat, sit down, shut up, and watch TV. We're cooking here!

Understanding the reason and source of our emotional responses is a cornerstone to better handling the situations and circumstances around us.

It might turn out that the strand that broke will simply get replaced, only to cause other strands to snap. I know I'm being abstract in this analogy, but what I'm trying to say is we are not the numerous ideas and experiences our ego makes these connections to. We are more than that. You are more than your emotions and beliefs.

You can shape your perception. Don't go off the rails with that. It's not an absolute truth. I'm a jerk remember; absolutes are only used for my convenience!

If someone hurts our ego, they've hurt our understanding of how the world is, the ideas we're connected to. It's painful, but it's a chance to analyze ourselves.

Why did someone saying, "Oh, you're getting fries?" make you think of your appearance? Why did the comment, "You're not really helping are you?" hurt my feelings? How do you view their opinion? Do you derive your sense of self-importance from them? Watch out for that kind of thinking! That's not how a jerk should think at all!

Do you believe they're trying to hurt, or help you? Why? How come

I get angry when my friend doesn't think my project will work the way I've envisioned it? Maybe they're right.

Stop putting people on pedestals above you. As a jerk, no one is above you. Jerk Rule #314.

However, there are pitfalls to this rule. Rabbit hole ahead! Some would say confidence is not the same as arrogance. If that were true, how come bad guys are so much cool in movies? They exude arrogance, and we as the viewers mistake it for confidence. Same difference for a jerk! Goody-goodies might inform you that the best leaders serve their followers. For a jerk, though, remember that independence is what we strive toward, not self-reliance.

They're foolish and wrong. We support others for our ends and not the wellbeing of groups. You know you do. Do you think we jerks are selfless? Ha, we want the credit!

Back from the rabbit hole, are there are opportunities to improve our perception skills instead of deflecting or lashing out? Jerks need to take care of themselves. No one else will. Did the person asking about those fries say it because he just got finished reading this jerk book and pulled out Jerk Rule #89? "Sarcasm works to make yourself and others feel better every time, all the time."

Perhaps they're just an abusive prick and should be dropped off your network. Or maybe it was just an innocent question. (Trust me—I read the fries comment multiple times. It can be said multiple ways using different inflections. It's hard to hold a Scottish Accent when saying the word fries!)

If you can look at your feelings, beliefs, and ideas as separate from who you are, you will find that you're able to take more positive actions.

But don't get it twisted—in order to be the best jerk you can be, emotional control and controlling your ego is paramount. You need to pick your battles wisely. If your mind is filled with conflicts of emotion, it will be hard to realize your goals. Even if rule #128 says emotions are the captain of your heart!

Stepping back from the short-term pain of interactions like these and evaluating why a web strand was tugged on or broken can build a stronger, more flexible web from that experience. We don't want to be too rigid as jerks, then we'll just be a ball of nerves.

What makes these strands so rigid?

Pride, the Best Quality... Or Something Like That

Pride cometh to us all... is that how that goes?

Pride is another confusing word, just like independence. I just wish we had some resource that gave us a clearer understanding of words. Jerk Rule #89 Sarcasm is awesome. Rules in action!

Let's talk about pride. Pride can be a good thing or a very bad thing.

Pride, as defined in the Oxford Dictionary, is *"a feeling or deep pleasure or satisfaction derived from one's achievements, the achievements of those with whom one is closely associated, or from qualities or possessions that are widely admired."*

It is also defined as *"confidence and self-respect as expressed by members of a group, typically one that has been socially marginalized, based on their shared identity, culture, and experience."*

Those sound nice, and we can label them the good kind of pride, but they don't make sense for those old sayings we are examining here. "Pride cometh before a fall," or that hugely successful book *Pride and Prejudice and Zombies* (Grahame-Smith, 2009).

These use the old English version of the word, defined as "excessive self-esteem." A synonym would be arrogance. This would be the bad kind of pride.

Wait... why am I telling you pride is a bad thing? You'd think a jerk would excel at being prideful.

Well, it's because pride creates noise. It takes your focus off your goals. Prideful people are weak-minded.

Yep, I said it. Arrogance is a weakness.

We'll be using both definitions of the word here, so I'll try to be clear on which context I'm using at the time.

I mentioned that we take pride in the ego web our spider creates. Both good and bad. Some strands we should take pride in. Our relationships come to mind (if they're not unhealthy). The fact that we work hard is something to take pride in.

But what should we watch out for? Pride in what we know. We should watch out for that, even the fact that we know we should watch out for it.

Ideas and concepts are dangerous things to take pride in. Why? Well, once again, they aren't you, more so even than how your relationships aren't you or your work isn't you. You can look at your relationships and determine the effort you put into them and the joy or motivation created from those interactions. With work, you can see the results from your effort.

But knowledge/ideas/concepts do not come from us. They are more like a shadow of something on a wall that we can point to. Of course, we utilize knowledge and ideas in many ways, and at that point, I would call that utilization "work" or "action." Calling an idea or concept yours without fully being able to grasp it, yet still taking pride in it, is dangerous.

You shouldn't take pride in anything but yourself. Again, I want to point out that you are *not* your ego spiderweb, you are not your thoughts. Nor do you need to listen to the instincts of the spider. I'll leave the question of "what am I, then?" for your own reflection. What do you think this is, a self-help book?

You can think of the bad pride as a process that solidifies the strands in this web. While it might seem like it makes you stronger, it really makes you fragile. I can snap prideful people like peanut brittle! And I do. It's my third favorite hobby after taking candy from babies and letting the air out of my friends' tires.

Intentional Web Breaking for the Good and Bad

Let me make something clear: everything without some form of moderation is terrible. If I could vote on creating a new scientific law, that would be a frontrunner.

Starting from that point, we can talk about what I call "Web Breaking." Recall that I mentioned "Ego Death" and how it didn't take Dr. Freud's definition seriously? I stand by my statement. Mostly out of pride, perhaps.

Jung spoke of psychic death. As I mentioned, these novel concepts lead one to talk about enlightenment and ascension. What I don't want you to glean from this section is that I believe there is any sort of enlightenment or spiritual awakening happening here.

I want to lean toward a functional understanding of things. I hate to use the term "self-help." I feel that's a fad term, like a diet you try for a few months and then toss away, only to gain all the weight back.

I've whimsically labeled this process as "Web Breaking ™" (pending... my procrastination and submission to the TM people.) Mostly because I have to think about PIGs (Passive Income Generators) so I might be able to retire off all the stacks of cash I'll get from it. Please don't let my selfish greed turn you off; if anything, you should sigh with relief. I'll be rich and you'll get a useful tool out of it. I'm just being my jerk self, after all.

This process, like all great revelations, isn't hard. It's simple, and because it's simple you might say, "yeah, I do that." I didn't say it was easy or even something you can do. It's a lie that people can do anything they set their minds to. A jerk said that. Your parents probably even said it. Chances are, six months from now, you won't be doing this. This is for the people who want change, not those of you who are content in your surroundings.

How do you know if you're content? Well think of it this way: Do you want to lose weight, but just can't seem to find the time? Barring a health restriction, that means you are content. Or, to be more accurate, that means you're not going to change. As a jerk in training, it's best to focus on something you can change or care enough to stop torturing yourself about.

If you don't care enough to lose weight, that's okay, but you need to stop telling yourself you *do* care because you're beating yourself up from the lies your shadow is telling you. People put action behind the things they care about. That's why many arguments are a waste of time, for both the participants and the audience.

I'm looking at you Facebook. #DownWithTrolls

Think about that: Without action, words mean squat. It's okay to waste other people's time as a jerk, but you should stop wasting your own.

Make a list of what you care about. Things in your life, goals. Not people. Jerk's don't really care about people. How much effort are you putting into figuring out how to do those things? If it's less than five minutes a day or week, you can probably go ahead and mark that off the list buddy. Find something you want to do.

As a jerk who loves to procrastinate, I feel I should tell you this. If you're not doing it today, you won't do it tomorrow. What's that annoying thing kids say these days? "Sorry, not sorry." That one lands right under "Whatever" and an eye roll on the annoying statements list.

Now that we both know about the things we care about, let's call out the process itself. Remember that analysis leads to paralysis. Everything in moderation.

Step 1: Spend Some Time with Yourself.

Can you do that? Fifteen minutes with no phone, email, games, or TV. Just you... and silence.

Some people call it meditation. They close their eyes and hum. I'm not saying you need to close your eyes and make noises. Humming can be soothing, but I'm not some guru from wherever gurus are found and marketed. Just stop what you're doing and sit with yourself.

This is important. While other people might not want to spend time with you, as a jerk, you should love it. You're awesome, after all, aren't you?

Step 2: ~~Quiet your mind~~ Grab One Thought

Got the first step down? Okay, good. Don't worry about "quieting your mind." That's impossible, like independence and proper sarcasm in writing.

The internet tells me the national science foundation and Deepak Chopra say people can have upwards in the range of 70,000 thoughts per day depending on what you focusing on. Sounds like a high-traffic area to me. How you can quiet a traffic jam? My best guess and belief is that it has to do with capturing them. Thoughts, not cars. Pretty sure car-capturing is just a cute way of saying grand theft.

By that math, we have around the low end of 600 thoughts within those fifteen minutes. Grab one.

Step 3: Ask Yourself Some Questions About It

What is it about? Why did you have it? What is it connected to? Is it meaningful? How so? Is it important? How do I address it? Are there other people involved? What are their projected thoughts on the subject (since they're in your mind, you'll have to think for them)?

Please note that "meaningful" and "important" are different things for all you tried-and-true analysts out there.

Yep, analyze your thoughts. Simple to say, hard to do. You need to really break them down.

I don't know about you, but when I get up in the morning, I end up taking on some of the most important global issues humans have ever come across. While I'm brushing my teeth, I aim to solve them, and naturally, I do (for the most part).

I have a great plan to stop global warming, or climate change if you're not a jerk. Just stop feeding beans to cows. Problem solved. Ice caps saved. You're welcome world. All Nobel prizes can be made out to me.

I also think about how if the hair on my ears grew as fast as the hair on my head, I wouldn't be balding. Such is life.

Step 4: Categorize the Thought

What am I doing with those global issues and minor ideas? They're important, for sure, but overall, do you think my keen insight in the bathroom mirror will ever be used to strike a peace treaty between Abu Dhabi and the warring country of Ys so we can get cousin Nermal back to the states? Even though the legendary artist Jim Davis has written extensively about this conflict in countless Garfield comic strips throughout the last three decades, it might go one for ages.

Probably time better spent brushing your teeth.

My daily thoughts on world peace may impress my friends, but I'm not supporting a charity or ending apartheid with them. These time-wasters can be cut out of your life; they might even be causing unnecessary anxiety.

What about more personal matters? My living situation, my rent, retirement. Why am I bored, or fat, or don't know how to talk to people?

Capture these thoughts. Tug on where they came from and why you tell or ask yourself these things. Drop the ones that don't matter. That's a great first step.

Stay there for a while. Write down what you learned. Did you learn anything? Probably that you have a lot of useless random thoughts popping up in your head. Now understand that everyone everywhere has both different and similar thoughts as you do. Everyone.

Step 5: How Much do You Know About the Thought?

This next step is a big one. Let's focus on what you know. How do you know it? What's it based on? Did you read a book, a blog, a comment, or just hear it? Is it a truth? How do you know it's a truth? Can you prove it or support it with evidence or simply explain it?

If it's a truth, what happens if someone disproves it (or attempts to)? Is it tied to something important, or can you accept a new view? Remember this is analysis—self-analysis. I'm trying to get you to think about what you're tied to, what you think is important, and why. If you don't know, then maybe it's not that important.

We're halfway through the process now.

Step 6: Drop it if it's Not Hot.

Are you willing to drop the time-filler thoughts? I don't mean thoughts about what you'd spend your lottery money on after you buy a ticket at a gas station. I mean the random nonsense.

I mean the thoughts your shadow brings up that you don't have an answer for. Thoughts that only serve to waste your time. Thoughts about going to the gym when you don't even care enough to sign up.

Drop it. You've already established through your actions (or lack thereof) that you don't care.

Instead, when you have one of those thoughts, tell yourself that you don't care. The shadow lies, so stop letting it lie to you.

We're almost done with this exercise.

Step 7: A Little Reflection on the World Around You

Conversations are hard. Everyone has similar thoughts, desires, home life, concerns, and worries. Heck, if we took all of our differences across the globe and listed them out, we might find we are more alike than we know.

Now arguments are a different type of conversation, a structurally more advanced type. Of course, depending on who you are and whom you're arguing with, the topic may be more juvenile. We won't talk about those arguments yet.

If you take time to understand your thoughts and what they mean to you, if you can explain them to yourself and how you are connected to them, then you can start to focus on other people's motives and concerns. It's simply the organization of your mind.

I'm not saying this reflection will make things hurt less when someone makes fun of you or works to change your mind, but analyzing your thoughts, how they make sense to you or how they could for others and why you have them will go a long way in helping you distinguish your thoughts from who you are.

Step 8: Stop Analyzing

Everything in moderation. This can be a great skill—one that you can utilize often, but don't analyze all your thoughts. Once you do this for a while, stop and relax. You get to accept that you've analyzed it. This goes for recurring thoughts, too.

Trust yourself. I don't mean in the abstract sense. You've analyzed it. It's done.

Give yourself space to acknowledge your analysis. If you're concerned about your judgment, ask others for feedback, but you ultimately need to learn to trust your own decisions somehow. This process can help, or to be "lawyery" about it, it may help you. Not definitive.

This can become sort of a "muscle memory" activity when you're alone with your thoughts or in a conversation with others. It's a great tool to have, but you don't need it all the time. If you do find yourself over-analyzing, stop.

Summary

Your ego is not who you are. I repeat, your ego is *not* who you are. Instead, think of your ego as a type of management system, or spider that connects your thoughts to various events or articles of knowledge in your life.

Your ego isn't alone. It is influenced by your Id and Shadow, which I use somewhat interchangeably, as well as the Superego. On top of that, your ego is pulling information from the physical world to enhance or adjust the webs it creates.

We sometimes conflate our understanding of ego to mean "us." When our ego is hurt, we tend to think of this as a personal attack. When one of our ideas is attacked or modified, we feel accosted. Try to remember that our ideas aren't us, even though we are connected to them. Sometimes these feelings are a correct response. Sometimes they are noise.

As humans, and especially as jerks, we need to understand that sometimes people simply want to hurt us. At other times, we become so attached to an idea or concept that we treat it with more concern than we do the person we're talking to. Relationships hang in the balance; your social network is in the hot seat!

Not all adjustments have to be negative. We need to understand our connection to our thoughts and ideas and come to understand other people's perceived connections as well. These ideas and connections are *not* who we are. Realizing this could mitigate many misunderstandings in the world.

Finally, you can use the web-breaking process as needed. But don't think of this as some enlightening technique or self-help fad, unless you can help me market it well enough to make me rich. Then, by all means, *do* view it that way.

This is simply a process to better understand your connections with your thoughts and feelings. Your ego helps to organize and categorize thoughts in your day-to-day life. It's your job to direct it. Your ego spider does not control you.

However, you should only use web breaking every so often, or you'll suffer from paralysis by analysis. You've been warned. Understanding our thoughts/beliefs/views helps us understand they are not who we are but rather only make up small aspects of ourselves.

Web breaking helps us to better acknowledge that while our thoughts and views may change based on others around us, our core self is growing from all of these interactions. Or it can grow if you choose to let it. Even jerks need to sift through the noise.

Jerk Rules

Jerk Rule #14: Trust no one. They're probably space aliens.
Pitfall: They might be aliens, and then this would actually be a great rule! Strike down your Lizard King Overlords! Wait... if you actually think there is a lizard King Overlord, don't strike them down. You're wrong, they're just people. You know, the stuff Soylent Green is made out of.

Jerk Rule #89: Sarcasm works to make yourself feel better every time, all the time. Sarcasm is always funny.
Pitfall: Some people see sarcasm as witty and smart. They don't take it as a cutting remark. Sarcasm could draw in people who want to be your friend. I know I've made a few that way! You've been warned! Remember, there are no pitfalls when using sarcasm!

Jerk Rule #123: Jerks should only believe what they can verify. Jerks don't need to verify what they say, only sound like they have.
Big Pitfall!: If you don't verify, people may find out and you'll turn into a troll!

Jerk Rule #125: You need thick skin to be a jerk.

Jerk Rule #128: Emotions are the captain of your heart!

Jerk Rule #167: Using abstraction or jargon that is unhelpful to the layman increases people's idea that you know what's going on.

Jerk Rule #178: Stick your nose into other people's arguments and offering your viewpoint is what people want you to do… They will love you for the assistance you're providing.

Pitfall: They may appreciate when you side with them, and it could lead to a lasting relationship. If you actually do research and have useful insight, people might start to see you as an authority and that means more responsibility!

Jerk Rule #314: Stop putting people on pedestals above you. As a jerk, no one is above you.

Pitfall: Putting people on pedestals can help you be more disappointed in them when they turn out to be human. Sometimes putting people on pedestals is helpful in your path to being a jerk!

Jerk Rule #315: Toilet paper goes under. According to jerk science.

We've talked about what our ego does. How it creates webs in the dark corners of our minds. How our feelings are connected to thoughts that we don't always give that much attention to.

Now let's take a look at how our ego manifests itself in the world around us. In our day-to-day lives, we approach arguments as though we are being attacked (or we are attacking other people). It's about winning and tigers blood. Thanks, Charlie Sheen, for that pop culture shout out.

To win every argument you're ever involved in you need to understand why you're arguing, how you're losing and what you're winning.

CHAPTER 7
WHAT IS AN ARGUMENT FOR?
WHAT IS ARGUING VS DISCUSSING? WHEN IS IT GOOD TO ARGUE? WHEN IS IT POINTLESS?

"When the debate is lost, slander becomes the tool of the losers."

—

Socrates

Socrates was a winner. He died from ingesting hemlock as a punishment for introducing thinking for yourself and thus corrupting the youth. (Sounds like a winner to me.) Maybe he should have presented his argument like a jerk... and not a "winner."

Who among us hasn't argued with a jerk or actually *been* a jerk in an argument?

Understanding how to argue and how not to can help us down the path to be the best jerk we can be. We don't just want to spout noise. We want to spout *believable* noise!

What is an argument? What does it look like? We see arguments on social media all the time, right? Or is that something different?

Just about everyone can communicate... at least on some level (though I know of chimps more adept at communicating than some, shoutout Washoe!). We manage to get around in this world because of this fact.

With today's technology, we can communicate across the world without leaving our houses or seeing anyone face to face. This is awesome, but perhaps it hinders our ability to hone these skills. We don't have to listen to feedback, and when we do, it's easy to misinterpret and ignore.

Let's start simple: Looking at the context of this chapter, what is an argument? Oxford defines it in a few different ways, but we're only going to use the first two definitions. We'll primarily stick with the second definition, even though the first seems to be the most popular approach on the internet today. Don't even get me started on Twitter.

The first, which is well known, is:

"an exchange of diverging or opposite views, typically a heated or angry one."

If you need an example, just dive into some Reddit boards or your vocal friend's political posts on whatever social media app they use. Now follow the comments. You'll run across an example of this first definition pretty quickly.

These "arguments" discuss politics/religion/current events seemingly to better the understanding of those topics for everyone reading, while all they tend to do is leave you with more questions. You'll probably notice some blowback—I mean, *feedback*.

The comment sections of the wild wild web are riddled with this noise. These types of surface arguments, quick memes, or statements, in my humble opinion, do nothing to further someone's point or draw your opponent to a certain side.

Rather, they act more like a breeding ground for breaking down solid arguments, creating divisive areas that hinder valid causes. They work to tear apart. Sorry, not sorry. If you have these "arguments" on the internet, congratulations. #TrollMagnet

They merely solidify people's feelings for whichever side they are on, to begin with. They offer divisiveness and not solidarity. There are many reasons for this, but naturally, we're only going to focus on ourselves. Why wouldn't we?

One reason is the ego. Again, people go into arguments believing they are tied to an idea or stance, and attacks on a point of view are an attack on who they are. As I've pointed out, only novice jerks believe their ideas are who they are. Thus, if we attack an idea, we are attacking that person.

This corrosive societal misunderstanding that we are our ideas is even propagated by those we might argue with. Everyone feels, at times, like they are simply the sum of their beliefs. But that's insane.

Standing up for what you believe in is important, but that doesn't require you to emotionally lash out. In fact, that could be detrimental to the cause you stand for. This first definition at times has also been given the label of a "fight;" while not ending in physical violence, it comes close enough and is just as damaging (if not more so).

The second way Oxford defines an argument is:

"a reason or set of reasons given with the aim of persuading others that an action or idea is right or wrong."

While both definitions are correct, I'm hoping to dive deeper into this second definition. I'm also squarely under the impression that Oxford has labeled this the second definition based on the (in)frequency of its use in our society. The fact it appears second saddens my verbose poetic stoic(Big "S") heart.

This world has got a pretty good handle on how not to learn anything from arguments. Social media arguments have become noise to people, and by utilizing the first definition in our public and private engagements, people just shut down. Which by the way, if you do engage in arguments, this way it is a tried-and-true path to solidifying your title as a jerk.

Even with the purest of intentions, arguing this first way lacks true motivation toward our definition. Without proper direction, you hinder progress. *Your* progress.

Chaos breeds nothing but chaos. Anyone who says differently is wrong. Regardless of your jerk status, you have to learn how to conduct yourself. That's why I'm laying out these rules for ya after all!

One way to properly argue is by knowing and understanding the rules of engagement and identifying a desired outcome at the start.

Only then can you purposefully break your opponent, and "win" more arguments. Although, on the Internet, people manage divisiveness just fine without this knowledge.

Let's break it down anyway for those of us who wish to do it with purpose.

When is it Good to Argue? Why is it Good at all?

We now know the definition of an argument. But when should we argue and why?

Arguing can be exhausting because people just don't know how to argue. They see arguments in three ways:

1. To get our way
2. To make our point
3. (or my favorite) Because it's Monday.

Those are the common answers in our heads or the amount of thought we put into these engagements before starting them.

Social media arguments demonstrate little concern about spreading misery, and that's because the 70,000 people "involved" in the discussion on the Internet have 70,000 different thoughts to contend and point to (or against).

As I said, chaos.

We can't always capture our thoughts, and many lack focus and goals in a day-to-day argument.

Guilty as charged. Put your pitchforks away.

Propagating confusion is certainly good enough for a jerk, and "winning" gives us a sense of power or strength. I'll talk about power later, but first I want to make an observation about arguing for the sake of power. It is an interesting and multi-layered concept that ranks up there with independence and pride.

Jerks should have these qualities, but we must also examine the pitfalls of not having them.

We like to assert ourselves, or at the very least be noticed. Arguing gives us this opportunity... if we're good at it. We feel our voices are heard when we argue or post comments that garner feedback. People love to feel heard; it makes them feel like they're part of something.

Arguing on social media is a spectator sport. Ninety percent of the time, our excellent and well-thought-out words won't change the other person's mind. Rather, our online arguments tend to be muffled by misunderstanding and instead confuse important issues.

If you're one of the many people that do this, thank you for your contributions. You are well on your way to jerkhood!

Other people's perceptions and experiences, combined with the complexity of communication through text, help compound the divisiveness and confusion.

God, it's great to be a writer! See what I mean? Yeah, I didn't think so.

Another awesome quality of the Internet argument is that our words are written in Internet stone (which might be better than writing them in actual stone). More terrifying, it means that others, years from now, can see what we've done in the name of truth, or "our truth."

That's a jerk way of saying "my opinion," and it means absolutely nothing, by the way, but many on the Internet live or die by that sentiment. As we're letting our jerk flags fly, we should only care about "our truth", we shouldn't care about *the* truth. It's Jerk Rule #43. #FactsAreLessimportantthanSelfExpression

Rarely do I recall any names of commenters from online discussions. Perhaps that's shocking to read, but neither can I tell you what the last argument I read online was or the noise that came out of it in the comment section.

Yet trolls and everyday people still desire to be noticed through their engagements, insults, and arguments. Arguing *does* give us a heightened awareness of this, though it's rarely remembered by the average person in their day-to-day. It's just more noise.

Now you could say trolls and cyberbullying are very impactful as they can lead to teenage (or even adult) suicide. The average person is looking to be heard and to "win" these little discussions online. (Note that cyberbullying falls squarely under asshole tactics and is not a jerk attribute.)

Ask yourself, what were the last seven arguments you had online, or read? What was the impact? Did you convince them, or do you even know? Do you care? If not, as a jerk why are you wasting your time?

The problem is that there is so much data in this information age—maybe too much—and so little to do with it. The average Joe forgets what he sees five minutes after seeing it.

With all this noise, many arguments don't present clear resources or obvious facts. They don't have to on the Internet. There isn't enough time. They read like opinions, but we regurgitate them as facts, or we read them as facts without understanding the supporting evidence. Both options are quite corrosive.

Let me make it clear: I'm not interested in opinions unless I ask for them. I want to hear facts and reasoning, like many of us do. This goes back to being heard and feeling that sense of power or belonging. I'll dive into those secrets later.

Personally, I would rather make a positive impact in someone's life than shove my understanding of right down their throat. Even as a jerk, I find this to be helpful, at least to me. It increases my power. As a jerk, I come first. Just saying, if you're going to be a jerk, you have to acknowledge when you're thinking like one.

Just like a multitude of others in the world, my sense of right is really just my opinion that I can't back up with supporting evidence. That's my fault. Don't get me wrong—truth is not relative, but it's okay if your "truth" is, as a jerk. Who cares about science, logic, and other people's facts?

You need to acknowledge what you don't actually know, even if you think you're the smartest person in the room. It's just stupid not to.

How do Arguments Happen?

Now most of us, me included, come into arguments when someone makes a statement or claim of some sort which we don't agree with. At that point, we're pretty quick to make it known we don't agree and then, in our endless magnanimity (read: generosity), provide the actual answer.

This, of course, is based on the infinite wisdom we have gained in our lives, which could be from experience, supporting facts, or perhaps random data we've heard and simply accepted as true.

While we can make good points on why we don't agree with someone else, I would argue that we might not be properly evaluating why we believe our side is correct, at least internally.

Do you ever ask yourself why you don't agree before commenting? It sounds like a normal thing to do when starting an argument, but do you actually do this? I certainly don't. I'm right, and I obviously don't need to prove it to myself!

We often quickly know we don't agree with someone, but we don't articulate why, outside of our feelings. Is this because the "other side" goes against what you currently understand?

You should be evaluating this. Otherwise, you're just a dumb jerk. Not just a normal jerk, but a dumb one.

Breaking Down an Argument

Let's pick a random topic to play with, like education and teachers getting more money in a merit-based system. That's a warm/hot button issue, right? And inline with something close to the School Stoppers' hearts. (And if you need a reminder, the School Stoppers' goal is enhancing the education system to support the needs of children, despite the confusion our jerk name might imply.)

There are multiple sides to this discussion, but let's just take a look at three. Also, for the sake of time, we'll simplify the arguments. That shouldn't be an issue, given how many simple-minded arguments you undoubtedly see every day.

Note that arguments can be as abstract or as complex as we want them to be. Jumping back and forth could help you "win." That's an important Jerk Rule (#50) to remember.

The first position calls to raise teachers' pay based on performance as a good, straightforward way to increase employee retention and boost the educational experience of students.

They would claim that teachers hold children's futures in their hands, so it goes to reason we should compensate them at a higher rate. At least pay them a comfortable livelihood to ensure they're able to continue teaching. Doing so will also make it an easier decision for students to become teachers instead of a fallback career choice.

If we don't increase their salary, there won't be as many teachers in the future, and the economy will suffer in the long run. That should be enough reason for raising teacher salaries. (Note how this simple point works for both merit and non-merit-based sides of the arguments.)

Next are those who believe that while teachers should be paid more, it shouldn't be based on a merit-based system, and a straight increase to the minimum base salary would increase retention and boost the educational experiences of the children.

While these two groups want the same thing, their arguments can and will differ. This side would also agree that an increase in salary would improve teachers' willingness to teach and overall increase the number of teachers.

However, they would say if it's a merit-based system, teachers, students, and the system may suffer from stress or outright fraud if teachers were asked to perform for compensation. For this reason, they argue, a simple base salary increase would be the safest way to ensure higher learning.

Last, for our purposes at least, there is a side that doesn't want to pay more school taxes, period. I might be simplifying that side for the sake of time, but I'm allowed. I'm the jerk here, after all.

This group could argue that parents control most of their children's futures. For example, if a child is home-schooled, they could get by or even exceed standards put in place by state and federal programs. Home-schooling can involve multiple households and teachers if you were not aware.

Another point for not raising salaries might be that it's not simply about shelling out money. Kids need to be taught, and in schools with bigger disparities in the teacher-to-student ratio, it doesn't matter how much teachers are paid. There is just not enough time, so raising salaries won't address the core issues, and money should be given toward equipment, books, and improving the curricula.

All these sides are *for* educating children but come at it in different ways. This adds a level of complexity to their arguments. The "why" and the outcome are no longer enough. Children are the future, after all.

Many of us operate on the "why" level of arguments when presenting our stance because if it's the right thing to do, the answer is easy. Why increase teacher's salaries? Because supporting our education system is right, and if you don't, you're wrong.

The "how" level is where this argument really should take place, and many people are not equipped with the information to engage in an argument at this level. We rarely come to arguments with solutions that can be transformed into action, and rarer still, solutions for the other side to or will consider. (One of the reasons it's so hard for politicians to agree. I mean apart from the systemic greed inherent in the political system... but I digress.) Without the "how," it's just more noise.

Let's step back, as a jerk, noise is helpful for us. Who cares if we create solutions, dissension and divisiveness give us room to operate! Still, let's walk through this before making it a useful jerk tool.

In this argument, it's vitally important to understand some of the logistics needed to increase salaries or where money should be placed in the system before simply adding your voice to the cause. It's great that you stand for something—it truly is. At least having the "why" gives you something to say. People might hear more than noise, and as a jerk, you want them to focus on your noise!

You can go around and shout about the "why," about the fact that children are the future and we should raise teachers' salaries, but if the "why" is your only contribution, your voice simply becomes as I've said, white noise. The real discussion, the argument, requires the "how."

I see many arguments that freely discuss the why but never the how. I'm continually impressed by how much time people can waste.

If you support something without the "how" and only share or yell about the "why," at best, you're only acting as a statistic. Unfortunately, nobody believes statistics anymore, and, well, you're just not helping. Sorry, not sorry.

At the worst, if you involve yourself in public arguments for the cause, you could come up against someone who has points you can't argue against. In that case, those who see your comments are persuaded to side against your cause because you can't properly defend against counterpoints you know little about. Shame on us forever doing this.

I'm not saying you should be afraid to speak up, but if you don't have some understanding from doing your own research, you're not helping the cause. Even if you feel and say you stand for it, you're likely working against it. Maybe that's fine for you. This is a guide to being a jerk, after all.

Citizens have a Right to Opinions!
And a Jerk's Opinion is Always Right!

If you back a cause based on an opinion or a feeling, that's acceptable. We all do this. However, you should understand that your opinion might rightly and truly be ignored if you use it in an argument. In short, though, if you don't have an understanding of the cause as a law-abiding "do-gooder," you should shut your mouth. Jerks need to buckle up and take notes!

Your opinion doesn't address the issues. An opinion is more like a feeling. A feeling of right/wrong or good/bad, no doubt, but starting an argument based on your opinion is a good way to confuse the issue for others. If you don't have rationale for your viewpoint, then it's an even weaker opinion.

As a jerk, I'm here to say that your opinion doesn't matter, but it *can* help you win!

That said, if you have an opinion on something, research it. This at least brings it into the realm of deductive reasoning. If I say that a unicorn is the result of a horse and a rhino getting frisky, that is my opinion, and it's wrong. Probably. Just like the flat earth theory.

If I say unicorns are mythical creatures made up in the mind of humans, but we could *make* one via genetic modifications using CRISPR technology, that's something that can be argued, even though it's not a complete argument with supporting facts. #AUnicornIsARhinoHorse

I don't mean reading a blog about it. You have to go deeper than that. Doing research shows you care about something. If you don't research it, should your ego web even connect a thread to it in the first place? Interestingly, it might anyway. Just make sure you understand where your opinion comes from before you give it to others.

Unless you're following rule #178, which is sticking your nose into other people's arguments. That's a viable path to becoming a jerk for sure.

As a rule, if you don't understand at least two sides of an argument, you probably shouldn't be involved. If this describes you, find a different way to engage people to feel heard. That's a solid non-jerk rule though, so be careful.

If you don't follow the teacher/salary discussion in the news, you might be surprised that there are teachers on all sides of it. It is a big, big world after all, even if Disney wants you to believe it's small. Everyone wants to have more money, but the "how," once again, is important. Without the "how," it's just more noise.

I listen to white noise when I go to sleep at night.

The Purpose of Arguments for Jerks (and Everyone)

Goody-two-shoes would say the real reason why and when arguments are important is to persuade and inform, not to prove that we're right or feel exhilarated or heard.

Remember! This reason doesn't apply to jerks. It applies to our goody-two-shoes opponent on the opposite side of the argument. Arguments are only important or helpful when the reason is to "set someone straight", or "put them in their place" with emotional force of will. #WinningMeansSubmission

So often in our technological world, we find arguments starting with an opinion. You know that "truth" we believe but don't know why. One backed by hearsay or some unknown source that hasn't been analyzed. If we don't understand why we have an opinion and can't articulate that, we shouldn't talk about it.

Otherwise, at some point, that argument or section of comments becomes a back-and-forth of venomous fighting for all to see. This causes harm, and harm as you recall is not something a jerk is really about. As jerks, we care for ourselves more than others, but harm crosses over the line into the asshole zone.

These arguments only work to entrench the opinions of others. It does not work to promote finding truth. Our truth, but still "truth". It's not an argument at that point; it's noise. Goody-goodies want to stop the noise. There might be some good news in that for us jerks.

Noise happens all the time, even inside of us because when someone attacks our belief, we feel they are attacking us. Recall the exercise for web breaking?

You might be asking yourself, how is it I'm not being personally attacked? If I have an opinion that I've researched extensively. If I point out this research to someone, and they say I'm wrong, how is that not an attack on my time, on my brainpower, on me?

Well, it is, if you think your personhood derives from your ideas, beliefs, research, and time. I'm going to say it again though: these things are *not* you. These things are what you've picked up over your life. These are things you do, not who you are.

I know I've gone over this, but you need to hear it again. I'm not saying you should roll over on your research and accept someone else's side when they present their case (provided their case is something with a foundation of research). I'm saying your "side" is not who you as a person.

When you feel like someone is attacking your beliefs or thoughts or research, you're right, but they are not necessarily attacking you—even if they think they are and they probably do. They could also be coming at the argument from a place of ego.

This concept that ideas are not who we are is a difficult thing to wrap our heads around. This isn't the case in fights. In a verbal fight, someone is for sure trying to attack you directly. Again, an argument is defined by persuading and informing.

Something that starts as an argument can easily devolve into a verbal fight or even a physical street fight when people believe they *are* their ideas.

Here's a cute little story. Some guy in Alabama shot his buddy because they couldn't agree over the height of James Brown. Let me say that again: a dude *shot* some other dude because they couldn't agree on the height of another dude.

He was 5' 6", by the way. I mean James Brown, not the guy who was shot. That took me five seconds to Google. They could have saved a bullet wound and an attempted murder charge if they'd bothered to look it up. Arguments are not an easy thing to maintain when people come at them from a place of ego.

When they devolve into a fight, whoever devolved it has logically lost their argument, no matter how many bullets they fire, hypothetical or otherwise. I guess Socrates was right.

How can we not bring our opinions into an argument? I already told you. Start breaking the webs your ego makes to the thoughts you don't have support for. Ask yourself why you have a certain opinion. And if you can't point to a source outside your own experience, it might just be an opinion.

You can "win" arguments or persuade other people solely based on your opinion, but that doesn't mean you're right. Remember jerks always want to be right. Jerk Rule #120.

Your opinion is not who you are, and more importantly, if all you give people is your opinions, you're not properly equipping anyone.

If you've started working on understanding where your thoughts come from and what is behind the things you stand for (utilizing the web-breaking strategy), then you might be ready for the next chapter. As a jerk, you have to protect yourself to be a better jerk!

Summary

Arguments exist to persuade and inform. Remember: you are not your ideas or your side of the argument. When people attack your "side," they are usually not attacking you, even if they don't know it. This is something you need to be aware of, even if they are not.

We need to properly detach ourselves from this ego web we've made. Why do we take arguments personally? It's this dual idea that opinions matter and that you are your opinions. Sure, if you're talking about ice cream and roller coasters, your opinions matter. Otherwise, they don't.

In an argument, your opinion just doesn't matter. Sorry, not sorry. When you bring opinions into an argument, you're conflating it, which can lead to misrepresentation and being a jerk. Perhaps we're on the same side of an issue, but if you can't properly articulate why you support something, shut up. You'll only hurt the cause.

As a jerk, you might not care, but if you stand for a cause, you have to research what you stand for. Not just blog posts on the Internets but actual books on the subject, articles, reports, and research papers. Know both sides. Join a debate club. Care or shut up.

If you're not willing to work, you don't really care. Sorry to hurt your feelings. Also, remember Jerk Rule #46: Apologize sarcastically. It's fun!

Or go the route of the many: the harmful. You can choose to believe you have an imaginary right to your fallible opinion. You can wield it like a club to smash the idea of having an actual productive argument that promotes thought and understanding and wellbeing for others. I like to watch movies and play video games to waste my time but to each their own.

Jerk Rules

So what did we learn about arguments and being a jerk?

Jerk Rule #43: The truth may set you free, but *your* truth is the only one that matters! #FactsAreLessimportantthanSelfExpression

Pitfall: If people start to realize your truth is not also true for them, they could also start to realize your truth isn't a truth at all.

BONUS Jerk Rule #46: Apologize sarcastically. It's fun for everyone! Or maybe just you. There is no pitfall for this rule!

Jerk Rule #50: Abstracting and complicating an issue when it's not needed can help you "win" more.

Pitfall: If you argue against someone who has done their research, you'll probably look like an idiot.

Jerk Rule #120: As a jerk, you should always be right. This means work to support what you think you know. Every morning, say into the mirror to yourself, "You are always right!"

Pitfall: If you don't do this, you might forget and think someone else has a point you didn't come up with first! And you might find out you're wrong!

Jerk Rule #178: Stick your nose into other people's arguments and offering your viewpoint is what people want you to do. They will love you for the assistance you're providing.

Pitfall: They may appreciate when you side with them, and it could lead to a lasting relationship. If you actually do research and have useful insight, people might start to see you as an authority and that means more responsibility!

What about the tools of the losers that Socrates was talking about? Okay, I get it—you want to know how to win an argument like a professional Facebook athlete saving the world one witty quip at a time.

In the next chapter, I'll go over some informal fallacies that you might run across in an average everyday argument. Knowing these fallacies will help you use them more effectively as a jerk or avoid them and point them out. You might even start to see these in arguments between people you consider "in-the-know." Let's take a look!

CHAPTER 8
HOW TO ARGUE LIKE A JERK

"Slander is just one tool for losers. Jerks have a whole toolbox!"

—

Alex D. Loch

Informal fallacies or errors in reasoning are the "losers' tools" Socrates despised. These are somewhat harder to point out than formal fallacies that deal with the composition and the overall structure of an argument. Addressing them in an actual real-time argument is an invaluable jerk tool. Jerk Rule #100: Know the fallacies of arguing, not to avoid them, but to use them to your advantage!

Informal fallacies naturally occur when someone doesn't understand how to articulate a particular stance in a discussion. Pointing out such fallacies is a good way to make it known that you're even worse than the guy who corrects people when they misuse the word "who" instead of "whom." (See also: my editor.)

By the way, it is "whom" if you can replace it with him or her, and it's "who" if you can use he or she. Easy-peasy. Didn't know you were going to learn valuable lessons, did ya?

You won't always want to point these out to others directly. Unless you're good at applying Jerk Rule #89 (sarcasm is always funny). In any case, I'll quote the honorable Mel Gibson: "Swing away, Merrill. Swing away," and break out the tools!

The Strawman had no Brain

The first fallacy I want to touch base on is commonly referred to as "the strawman." It is mostly used to either confuse the audience or confuse their opponent on an issue. That is to say, as a jerk would use it.

You might also see this fallacy occur when your opposition doesn't fully understand the side of the argument you are on. I could see this being used in conjunction with the ad hominem or loaded question fallacy (more on those later) at some point in the argument as well.

So what is it, exactly?

The strawman is named so, as your opponent will frame your side of an argument in a slightly different context that is easy to deconstruct, knockdown, or burn with the vengeful fire of the argumentation gods.

Recall the group that argued that parents do most of the future-holding and not the teachers? They might claim that since a teacher's influence is minimal in terms of time together and lessons are not as well-remembered past grade school, teachers aren't impactful enough. Thus, funding should be directed toward homeschool efforts over increases in salaries as kids remember teaching moments with their parents more.

While it's true that parents often spend more time with their children than teachers, this statement is overly simplifying a student's relationship with their teachers. It should be stated that these relationships cannot be properly compared with time alone.

The strawman fallacy sets up a simplified and inaccurate argument for the opposing side that they can later refute in the argument. That way, essentially, they are winning an argument that they themselves have established rather than the opposing side's actual view.

This is one of the reasons you should understand both sides of an argument. At the very least you'll know what you're arguing for. If you don't catch this fallacy, you might walk away thinking your argument is wrong when it is not. You could also find yourself wasting time discussing non-sequiturs (which literally means "it doesn't logically follow").

Fallacy of Authority

The next fallacy takes a reference from a source that only amounts to an opinion of that source/person. If the source is well known, famous, or seen as an authority of some type, their statements can be misconstrued as facts.

This is called the argument from authority, or the fallacy of false authority. In these cases, remember that even if someone from authority says something, that doesn't make it true.

To properly use an authoritative source, make sure that the source provides evidence and is not merely stating an assumption. Know the evidence behind their statement to use it in an argument.

Let's take the argument that without electricity, we wouldn't have the technology we have today. You couldn't claim that as a fact that simply because Benjamin Franklin said, "Electricity is the wave of the future."

You would need to support it by referencing events throughout time such as the creation of the telephone, computers, and the impact of having electricity creating advancements for us. Simply because old Ben said it doesn't mean it is so.

By the way, I made Benjamin's quote up. He didn't say that, as far as I know. It's just an example... also, it's a good example of not believing everything you hear and read.

The Loaded Question Fallacy Trap

This next one is great. It's something you *must* put in your tool bag if you're going to be a tool... er... jerk.

Loading up your questions is a must. It's not just a fun game for the family! Some examples of loaded questions sound rather direct, but within it lurks a hidden assumption that your opponent hopes you will not address. Such jerks!

They are, however, still detectable. Let's do a simple one: if someone asked you, "Given that welfare supports those who can't work, how could someone be against it?"

This is a loaded question as it clearly states that welfare supports those who can't work. Furthermore, it assumes that if you don't support welfare, then you're on the side that is attempting to hurt those that can't work.

Answering this question directly gives the opponent and your audience a sense that you agree that welfare supports those who can't work, and it ignores the underlying implication that not supporting welfare is the same as not supporting those who can't work.

A way to disarm this type of question is to address the assumption within it first. Something like, "Well-fare does support those who cannot work, which is its purpose. It is also true that others who can work take advantage of the system. This is what I am against.". You could then follow up with an explanation of why you wouldn't support it being taken advantage of.

A non-loaded question would simply ask, "How could someone be against supporting the welfare system?" This makes no assumption and simply asks a direct question—perhaps even disarming an opponent to allow for a debate that gets at the heart of the issue rather than engaging in a subtle ad hominem (more on this later) and the creation of noise around the program.

The "Everyone's Doing It" Fallacy

Another classic fallacy that doesn't hold up and shouldn't be allowed to is the "Well, everyone else is doing it, so it must be right!" argument. I'm not going to talk about the similar tu quoque ("you too") fallacy, but it relies on the same assumption. This is also known as "ad populum" and can help jerks sound smart for no good reason.

Kids use this rather frequently... and maybe I use it frequently, too. "I should be able to do it because Johnny and Mary get to."

Just because a group of people supports the argument does not mean the premise is valid; this is similar to the authoritative fallacy in that way. Many times, your parents would counter this with the classic comeback, "If all your friends jumped off a bridge, would you do it, too?"

But the joke's on Mom and Dad because bungee jumping is a thing. In fact, bungee jumping off a bridge is the reason I wrote this book in the first place. The doctors say my head trauma is permanent and I shouldn't be writing *anything*, but what do they know?

That bridge question is logical in this sense, but it's not helpful if they should be talking to you about the dangers of drug addiction, which can destroy your future, all for a small chance to feel a certain way or fit in. Drugs are not the same as bridges. Remember that. Drugs are bad, m'kay?

The Two Options – The "No Waiting" Fallacy

This leads me into our next fallacy, an either/or type assumption in an argument. Let's take the drugs from our last fallacy. This discussion has some either/or properties to it, right?

For quite a while, we've waged a war on drugs. It's been going incredibly well. (Sarcasm is fun! See?) Drugs kill. You've seen what it did to that egg, right? For this false dilemma fallacy, we'll revisit my premise from the last paragraph of the previous section.

I mentioned that drug addiction is dangerous and could destroy your future. That's true, but the assumption one could make is that doing drugs (I'm referring to hard drugs like Walter & Jesse's crystal blue meth or any of Ben & Jerry's ice creams) will instantly make you addicted. In reality, it's based on multiple factors we don't fully understand, including genes, environment, and age.

In other words, you could become addicted after one use, or it might take multiple uses. If you're frequently around drugs, statistically chances of addiction go up. The younger you are, while your body and brain are still growing (up to age twenty-five), the harder the drug, the easier it tends to be to develop an addiction.

That's not to say that trying heroin at age fifty means you'll be able to use it without getting addicted!

The false dilemma fallacy in the drug war argument stemmed from stating that people wouldn't be able to function if they used drugs. It actually may have helped give rise to drug use, because people tested the theory and proved it wrong.

If you're told taking something will kill you, and you see other kids taking it and not dying, it takes some of the wind out of the argument. But people use this fallacy all the time! What D.A.R.E and similar programs worked to explain was how drugs, over the long term, affect your life and opportunities. Low self-esteem, peer pressure, and this either/or mindset were what D.A.R.E fought against to varying successes.

If you present a false dilemma and that dilemma, in turn, is proven untrue, you run the risk of your entire position falling flat and people using drugs around the world and fueling a criminal empire of drugs, sex workers, and human trafficking. Well, maybe not with every argument, but that certainly happened with this one.

Always research your arguments first, and stay away from false dilemmas. Unless you're sure you are going to get away with it. Most people don't fact-check properly, and fact-checking sites sadly are not always reliable sources, even if they come from a place of "authority."

That's a Slippery Slope Fallacy

Since we're still talking about drugs, let's mention the slippery slope fallacy. It's similar to the false dilemma but different.

In the false dilemma, I said that doing drugs will cause addiction. While it's statistically true that doing drugs increases your chance of addiction, logically it's not the case in all situations and could lead to me losing the argument under those pretenses.

The slippery slope fallacy goes something like this: If someone smokes marijuana, the gateway drug, those people will start using harder substances. So people shouldn't use marijuana.

Let me say this: in your younger years, before twenty-five, your brain is still developing. You shouldn't use mind-altering drugs. That's just truth.

It doesn't change the fact that you *can* use them. I won't stop you. I don't even know you. I'm just sharing what I know with you.

Moving past that PSA, marijuana isn't a gateway drug. Rather, adolescence is a gateway *period* in our lives. We are more susceptible to peer pressure. We want to fit in and be liked (the popular path) or escape for some reason (the unpopular path).

If you want to stop your kids from doing drugs, or at least give them the tools to not live as drug addicts, don't use this fallacy in your argument against drugs. Show them what a drug addict looks like or lives like. Teach them what drugs do to your body.

Please note, it's not going to the kitchen and frying a freaking egg. If that's your plan, you should just hand them a pipe yourself.

The slippery slope fallacy uses fear as a point against something, while that fear might have some founding evidence if it promotes a leap in logic and isn't presented correctly to properly support an argument you might lose in the long run. You can use this fear as a jerk, but make sure someone doesn't see you use it!

The Correlation Means Causation Fallacy

Enough about drugs—let's talk about the correlation/causation fallacy. To give an example of this, let's take a hypothetical writer's work schedule. Say he gets up every day at nine in the morning for a year, has a cup of coffee, and checks his apps. After the morning ritual, he sits down and writes for four hours.

Let's say he writes a book that first year, and in the second year he starts the same routine, but he gets up at ten and forgets his coffee. This, in turn, causes him to waste more time checking his apps, and he doesn't finish his second book in the next year.

The writer then must explain to his agent or publisher that he didn't finish his book on time. The reason, he says, is he got up later and didn't have his coffee. This took away his app-checking schedule, which was like a timer giving him fifteen minutes to browse the news. Without it, he didn't spend as much time writing in the afternoon.

This, of course, is the writer's causation fallacy, not to mention some issues with a high external locus of control, which we won't go into.

His changed schedule and lack of drinking coffee doesn't equate to sufficient supporting evidence for not finishing his book on time. There could be multiple factors that are unaccounted for here.

To properly show causation, one must look at all possibilities or at least examine several other possibilities. Such as crippling anxiety due to social interaction, imposter syndrome, alcoholism, all the other stereotypical aspects of the life of a writer and their tortured souls, as well as the death of his dog may have prevented his focus.

Just remember that the correlation of a group of events does not mean those events were the root of the issue. You need to properly research other cases to not get caught in such a fallacy or adjust your argument accordingly.

The Peace-Keeper Fallacy

Moving forward, another fallacy is the middle ground or false equivalence fallacy. To show the logical flaw in this assumption, let's be hyperbolic.

The Earth is a sphere-ish shape—or at least some of us believe that. Another rogue group of people with mind-bending imaginations claim it is flat. Thus an argument exists between the two sides.

To promote acceptance, or in the name of peace, we could say the two sides should settle on the Earth being cube-shaped. Problem solved everyone gets what they want. It's got flat sides for the "flatters" and three dimensions for the "spheries." (I'm sure those pet names will stick.)

This fallacy is the compromise between something true and something false. If we're being honest with ourselves, jerks, or not, this is something we shouldn't accept. When dealing with science and truth, the middle ground is not something we can stand on. The middle ground is shaky ground.

The Big Burden of Proof Switch-Up Fallacy

Let's talk about a fallacy that some people don't quite get: the burden of proof. This sounds pretty straightforward, right? So how do we manage to confuse it so often? In an argument, the burden of proof always, *always* lies with the person making the claim.

For example, say you're arrested for a crime. It's the responsibility of the state to prove your guilt in a court of law. They are the ones bringing the argument against you.

That's pretty straightforward, but in everyday arguments, it gets fuzzy. I can't say that something exists simply because you can't prove it doesn't and consider myself correct. The burden is on me to prove it exists, not on the other side.

The burden of proof is always on the one who made the claim/charges or is challenging the status quo within an argument. Shifting that burden of proof does not automatically prove your side. Plus, it's just lazy.

The Eye has an Eye Fallacy

Similarly, instead of shifting proof, you should not shift the process to validate an argument. The Homunculus fallacy does this well. It's described with the following example.

Looking at the process of how we see things. If we view the world through our eyes, something inside of our eye looks at those images to interpret them.

What this explanation does is avoid explaining the process of "seeing" while seemingly reaching the desired end. That "end" is explaining how we see things, or how that "something" inside us sees things.

In other words, it moves the process that is to be explained to a different level, thus avoiding the actual discussion to be had. This is not the same thing as abstraction, but in using and looking at abstraction this fallacy can be found.

Ad Hominem

Finally, my favorite form of fallacy! I see it all the time, everywhere. Ad hominems creep into arguments when we can't properly defend a point, oftentimes one we believe is so intrinsically woven into the being of who we are.

Someone smart might say it's our egos trying to protect their belief systems at the expense of another without proper research. You can find this happening on Facebooks and Reddits all around the internets.

A lot of people employ this fallacy because they don't understand how an argument is won or know enough about their stance to provide support for it.

With that mindset and limited understanding, many of us, me included, can fall into this fallacy by attacking the person and not the argument. This is not how arguments are "won" by the goody-two-shoes of the world. This is the perfect fallacy for an up-and-coming jerk in training.

But it's the Same! The False Equivalency Fallacy

The final example I want to mention is one of words. I'm an author, so it seems fitting. I also love saying things that can be taken two different ways. Sometimes it shows intelligence. Sometimes it's comedic. But in an argument, the fallacy of equivocation is not as amusing.

When you use a word or words that have two meanings within the same argument, that's a false equivalence fallacy. I found a similar example (which I reference in the appendix), but I've updated it here because it's my unnatural right as an author to do so.

Suppose you have a meeting tomorrow. You might use this argument on yourself.

"I'm an adult and have a 'right' to do what I want," you assert. "By that logic, it's 'right' for me to go skateboarding tonight at the park and not prep for the meeting tomorrow."

Just because the word "right" is used correctly in the initial premise, it doesn't follow that it's right to use another definition of the same word in the supporting clause. It brings confusion.

If your opponent can't understand your side of the argument due to the obscurity of the changing definitions within the words you use, (albeit my explanation was quite simple) you can't claim that as a victory. Even if it's "super fun" to watch them fumble over your intended meaning.

In other words, define your terms upfront. That way there's no ambiguity on the back end.

This fallacy can confuse, and while as a jerk this may be comical, it's not all that helpful.

What Does it Mean if I See One of these Fallacies?

Remember: just because an argument contains one or multiple fallacies doesn't mean it isn't valid or that the claim is wrong. It just means the other side doesn't know how to properly argue for it.

Which in turn means it's a waste of your time and the potential audience's time, who sadly will most likely take portions of the argument and use them in follow-on arguments. Like spreading a virus. As a jerk, it's great to know you can waste someone's time, but use these fallacies wisely.

You can't "win" an argument like this, as the other side cannot properly present its case. Or the fallacy may be identified down the road and the entire argument might be thrown out by future audiences, even if good points were made. That said, we jerks can still make use of these tactics.

If you don't want to take the time to understand your side of an argument, these fallacies might be your best hope in hiding your incompetence. This is a guide for jerks, after all. Using these as tools in an argument would categorize you as one for sure.

Jump into the conspiracy rabbit hole with me for a minute. With these fallacies, you could see and say that they work to corrode and corrupt our view of sources of truth into relative truth. In this technological era, the unprecedented speed of communication has served to strengthen our ability to act while allowing anyone to say or promote anything.

Relying on AI algorithms and media sources to propagate truth based on the bottom dollar has weakened our ability to trust. This has divided us as people of the world. Maybe that's true, or maybe it's "true".

Who knows? I'm just teaching you to be a jerk, and these fallacies will help ensure that. What's a little lie gonna do? Destroy human civility and etiquette? Yeah, right.

Summary

Recall the tools for the "losers," as Socrates would say. We discussed what we can use in these daily arguments to tear each other apart, cause divisiveness and confusion. Who needs unity among us? All for one, I say. Me.

Knowingly or unknowingly, we use these tactics to "win" arguments. Remember, if you want to be a jerk, you need to want to "win" arguments by defeating your opponent for all to see. You should never engage in an argument hoping to seek the truth, especially if the truth is on the other side.

Jerk Rules (and Tactics)

Let's not forget about the crucial Jerk Rule presented in this chapter:

Jerk Rule #89: Sarcasm works to make yourself feel better every time, all the time. Sarcasm is always funny.
Pitfall: Some people see sarcasm as witty and smart. They don't take it as a cutting remark. Sarcasm could draw in people who want to be your friend. I know I've made a few that way! You've been warned! Remember There are no pitfalls when using sarcasm!

Jerk Rule #100: Know the fallacies (tactics) of arguing, not to avoid them, but to use them to your advantage:

Jerk Argument Tactic #1: Strawman – No Brains!

Jerk Argument Tactic #2: Argue from Authority – But Billy said… and he's in 6th grade!

Jerk Argument Tactic #3: Loaded Questions – With sour cream and chives!

Jerk Argument Tactic #4: Bandwagon – Everyone's doing it!

Jerk Argument Tactic #5: The False Dilemma – Danger! Stop! Cliff ahead!

Jerk Argument Tactic #6: Correlation/Causation Fallacy – Coffee rules your life!

Jerk Argument Tactic #7: Middle Ground – Peace and confusion for all!

Jerk Argument Tactic #8: Burden of Proof – Flip it like a cup!

Jerk Argument Tactic #9: Personal Attacks/Ad Hominem – The easy way!

Jerk Argument Tactic #10: The Slippery Slope – Thin ice!

Jerk Argument Tactic #11: Equivocation – Right-handed people are right!

Now that you're an expert at how to evade and turn arguments to your advantage using these fallacies, let's turn to why we would want to do such a thing. Power. Ultimate cosmic power!

Err, I mean, just regular power... but as jerks, we take what we can. Everyone wants power, but if you don't know what it is, you're never gonna get it. Do you want it?

CHAPTER 9
WIELDING POWER

*"Power resides where men believe it resides.
No more and no less... a shadow on the wall...yet shadows kill."*
—
Varys, A Clash of Kings - *George R.R. Martin*

Knowledge is power, strength is power, money is power, power is power. What is power?

Power is an elusive idea, some say it has roots in knowledge, others say strength. Money commands power. The people with the money make the rules. Or perhaps power lies with the rule-makers... or does it reside within the individuals of a society or group?

The first definition of power in Merriam-Webster's dictionary is:

"the ability to act or produce an effect."

That makes sense. People with power get things done, but it doesn't help to understand how people come to power, but what power is. That's one reason people argue—they feel it gives them power. In certain ways it does, but this is oftentimes instantly wasted on your spider. Sorry... your *ego*.

After the argument is over, the potential for this thing we call "power" can be reduced in scope to mere feelings within ourselves and others that eventually dwindle to nothing—to noise. Many times, these feelings and thoughts are abusive or corruptive. That translates to pride for our ego if we win or negatives for our shadow to bring up to us if we lose. Neither of these are lasting.

The goody-two-shoes of the world focus on promoting change or truth, not gaining power from arguments. Arguing to get that rush of feeling "power" or "winning" is the good stuff for jerks. While our goal doesn't help create lasting power (as we're going to come to understand it), it can give us a great rush!

Let's look at the definition of power from another standpoint. Perhaps that will help give us insight into how one comes to a position of "power."

Power in science (physics) is said to be: "the rate of energy transfer or work done divided by the delta or time range."

This gives us a single unit of power. If we take this unit to carry the meaning of the Webster definition of power, we get a single unit capable of acting or producing an effect. More work produced in a shorter amount of time means the units of power increase in size or "effect."

But we're not machines. We don't view power as something individuals create, but something they have. I say there is a flaw in how we view power when it comes to people "controlling" power or "controlling" anything really.

Know this: You are not in control of anything but yourself. Jerk or not. Know it.

Sorry, not sorry.

We say someone commands power, respect, or authority, but perhaps power isn't something you have to command at all. In this chapter, I'm going to break down power into what I believe to be a manageable, tangible concept that we can grasp and use.

As a jerk out for only yourself, that should be awesome news. Beware the pitfalls, though. I'll point 'em out for you as we go.

This new view will shed light on how you as an individual can utilize what is sometimes seen as the "end-all-be-all." Others less inclined to be jerks would say that "power" is merely a means to another beginning and not a prize to obtain. Hokum! Malarkey! Balderdash! Nonsense!

In the quote written by George R.R. Martin, Varys talks to Tyrion Lannister about power. Varys speaks in a riddle about a sell-sword and wielding power over life and death. He spoke of the power of kings calling on stronger men. Finally, the conversation ended on power being a shadow, one that Tyrion himself could cast.

Before I get into breaking down the idea of power, I want to tie this back to our previous discussions on the shadow. What does it mean to cast a shadow?

In the context of *Game of Thrones*, I enjoy the conversation ending on abstraction or the metaphor of power. Power as (is) a shadow. I think it's well written and speaks volumes about the aspects of this abstract concept known as "power."

Back to the Shadows. Sing it with Me!

Varys is explaining to Tyrion that even though he's small, his presence and words reach far out in the world of fire and ice, just as any (wo)man can. Interestingly, a shadow is a pretty good analogy for power in this regard. A shadow can become bigger or smaller, covering anything it touches. It's very poetic.

Let's go back to science for a minute. I like to understand the functional side of things. It helps ground our ideas. How does a shadow grow? By object producing the shadow coming closer to a source of light. In growing, the shadow also becomes more blurred at the edges.

Varys is explaining that the closer he gets to the throne, the more power he can hope to have. I take it Varys, as the Master of Whisperers, thinks rather highly of the power he believes he commands. The shadow Varys is referring to is, of course, influence. Influence is where true "power" lies.

Tyrion then asked an excellent question: he asks if power was a mummer's trick. Power, as it's become to be known, is a trick in and of itself. The perception of power being tied only to those who know how to use it is part of that trick.

Now as I'm sure you know, to be the jerk with the power you have to *steal* the power sword from He-Man to obtain the Power of Grayskull!

Wait... no. I mean you need to combine and apply the tools I've already gone over to be able to utilize "power" to the best of your jerk abilities. Web breaking, understanding fallacies, following the great rules in this guide.

Breaking Down the Idea of Power

We can now break down how this abstract idea of "power" actually works. Along the way, I'll point out a few physics formulas that make the overall abstract idea of power more functionally understandable... but not to mechanize it and make it seem cold. We are discussing psychology, your relationships, self-esteem, and success as a jerk, after all.

However, if we can grasp this rather cold de-glossed version of "power," maybe it won't seem so... unattainable. This gives us an algorithm for power!

Simply stated, I'll explain how I've utilized these abstract connections in my day-to-day path to jerkhood to become more... "powerful.".

Let's start with the heavy hitter, using the physics formula for power itself. Keep in mind, I'm not a physics major, nor do I have a background in it. I'm an internet/YouTube-watching guru and use information as I see fit. What jerk doesn't? Here's the formula:

p *(power)* = w *(work)* / Δt *(delta time)*

Let me try to translate these hieroglyphics for you. Shouldn't be that hard.

You can read this formula as "Power is equal to some idea of work divided by a range of time." That's what "delta time" means—a range of time. You can imagine the range of time is when the work started till the time it finished. We can show it like this:

Δt = tf *(final time)* − ti *(initial time)*

We can do the same thing for w *(work)* in that formula, but we don't need to make this more complicated. For now, just know that work is a variable of your effort.

Therefore, the amount of power you have is a product or the outcome of your work over the range of time taken to perform that specific task. So, simply put, power is a measure of work done in a span of time. That's easy enough to grasp, but it's quite different than how we might think of influence and how it works. Yet it is still one and the same.

I didn't want to gloss over it but it's scary for sure! Almost instantly we find work is involved! So we have the physics formula for work:

w (work) = *f (force)* times *d(distance)* ...

To say this in real words, work equals a person's impact (*force*) times the reach (*distance*) of that work or the breadth of what that impact entails.

We'll ignore anything after the three dots for our purposes here. At least until we get a physicist on the writing staff at the School Stoppers publishing house... in which case I'm sure they'll want to rewrite this entire chapter.

Now the idea of *f (force)* is not the same as power in physics.

f (force) = *m (mass)* times *a (acceleration)*

For our translation purposes, this says: The amount of force (think of this as "impact") is found from everything a person is and what they currently possess times their ability to be motivated. That's what force is; that is the formula for impact. Not too bad, right?

I want to flesh out this algorithm a little more. *m (mass)* should be interpreted as how much you know—your relationships, knowledge, and talents. How adherent your friends are to your ideas. Your skills and experiences.

That's what your mass is. Everything you are. Your initial starting capital, let's say.

Acceleration is motivation. It's the implementation of your skills and your network's abilities. It's your attitude, and it is greatly affected by your shadow and self-esteem. I mean, they're practically roommates. That means your shadow and self-esteem directly affect your impact, i.e. f (*force*).

Working with the tools and questions we mentioned earlier will go a long way for you here. Jerks might not be likable, but who says they can't get things done?

For something that does not have acceleration/motion, think motivational attitude and drive; it does not have force, no matter how much knowledge/network it has. Or, poetically put, if you're not doing something, you cannot hope to have an impact.

I appreciate the synchronicity of the formula and the ancient uncommon wisdom behind it. I hope it's coming together for you.

Now you're probably thinking, "You're telling me that to be a powerful jerk, I have to have a positive attitude?"

No, that's not what I said. I said "motivational attitude." Having a positive attitude is for the goody-goodies out there. As jerks, we want to get things done. Our things. You should have a positive attitude about that; a jerk should enjoy their own company. And chances are you won't have many friends in this line of work.

A motivational attitude allows you to do so much more than a positive "self-help" attitude. Jerks everywhere should embrace this. Careful, though—that involves some web breaking. It could lead you to act like a better person, but as long as it's only an "act".

To make sure you motivate properly. If you wave your hands around and raise your voice at strange times you can get people to respond to you quicker than a soft and calming tone. It's fun to watch people jump up and run around like ants! Just try not to get a big head about it, assholes do this too. You want people to be motivated to help you, not plot against you and steal your sandwiches. I've lost many a sandwiches getting this wrong. #SandwichThievesUnite

Life secret: sometimes being positive can be a negative. I don't know that there's a formula for that, but I'll go into that later.

Now that I've broken down what science says about power, how does that help us?

It gives a framework. Abstract ideas are supposed to provide at least that. As a journeyman jerk, keep note that abstraction can be useful in reducing work, and therefore enhancing power for oneself. It's Jerk Rule #28 in the handbook. Tuck that one in your pocket.

The gap between abstraction and implementation is understanding, just as it is between arguments and logic. You know what power is now, its influence, and how your work affects it—starting with what you bring to the table and your motivation.

Now let's talk about the relation to creating an implementable concept of your potential for gaining "power" in this world.

People are Objects

Within the force equation, you are the "m" for mass. I'm not doing a fat joke. I pointed out that was you and what you have in terms of resources and skills. Except that's not really what the formula says.

For this section, we'll need to go back to the definition. Know that mass is the size of an object in the force equation. That object happens to be you. That's right you're an object. I said it!

We treat other people like objects all the time. Hopefully, that doesn't shock you. Jerks should know this already. If it makes you feel more comfortable, say they're objects only when they aren't around, when we don't think of them.

Don't worry, that doesn't mean you're a jerk per se—although that's what I'm trying to help you become.

We are naturally busy and limited in scope as we go about our day. Maybe we don't do this intentionally or with ill will, but for many of us, we are focused on ourselves. We have concerns about our immediate and secondary circles of friends and family. Outside of that, people exist, but they exist like any other abstraction.

Out of sight, out of mind.

If it wasn't this way, our chances of generating work or changing aspects of our lives slopes downward or upward drastically. This slope depends mostly on how many tasks or people we have to manage/relate to within our lives. (Another good thing web breaking is for is helping focus.)

Another way to say this is that we are more helpful and capable when we can focus on a few things. Feel better? Good, I'm glad... I guess. Even if I am only an object to you.

That said, we should always look to increase our social networks and knowledge. This ties into our mass in that cold formula from before. This increases our potential for "power" as an expansion of responsibility and knowledge increases so does the amount of work we can perform.

The Shadow and the Unreliable Teacher that Steal our Force

Speaking of objects, in this age, we are inundated by all of the events and people outside of our control. This can cause anxiety. Perhaps this is why some things seem to get worse when we can't focus on helping just those around us. The pressure of all the problems of the world begins to weigh us down.

Gotta love technology. It's powerful. It's productive in how it can push and pull us together. It's destructive in how it can break us down. Just like an asshole... Both kinds.

Under this noise of life, growing our personal networks and knowledge to best increase our ability to perform work with greater ease is sidetracked. When we lose focus, we lose our force in this world. I explained that without force, we can't hope to have an impact.

Let me end this section with this advice: To increase your impact, you must increase your knowledge in your various interests and build your relationships. You can use jerk tactics to keep your friends under your thumb or fall by the wayside with the goody-goodies to "support" and "care" for one another.

This ties back to how we see and view ourselves. If we allow our shadow and the world to push us around, creating noise, our drive, our impact is affected. If you want to be a "powerful" jerk, you have to work at maintaining focus. There are no free rides, even for those who want to get ahead for free.

The Great Lie Overshadowing the "Golden Rule"

"Treat others how you would want to be treated." Or pick a variation of it. I'm here to tell you, that's a goody-goody rule. Thankfully the "Golden Rule" is complicated, just like other words we'll touch on later. This causes more confusion, and so people don't follow the rule as they should.

Just imagine if everyone followed this rule for its true intent. Oh, man! What a nightmare! Then who would I be able to project my negativity onto?

As I said, thankfully while the one rule to rule them all says we should treat others how we want to be treated, some of us don't treat ourselves very well. Therein lies the problem, and as jerks, misery appreciates company...

I mean, we still don't want to harm anyone like an asshole, but sometimes making someone have a bad day provides us with some extra pep in our step! Am I right?! #JerkPep

People forget that the golden rule also says, "We need to love ourselves as we should be loved, not necessarily how we are loved." I'm not sure how long the golden rule is, but I think that's all of it. This "addendum" to the golden rule is also something that's glossed over from the noise generated in our lives. It's also good news for jerks everywhere. Love yourself!

The world does not have time and does not love, just like our shadow does not have our best intentions at heart. They steal your ability to make an impact, to have "power." We cannot look to the world for confirmation or adoration before loving ourselves.

Amateur jerks say, "Well, once I get respect, I'll give it."

You'll never give it, then. The world will never care for you to the degree you want it to. The world will, however, point out your negatives rather quickly and easily. I'm talking about all the trolls and assholes out there and the negative bits our shadows have stored from the terrible things it soaked up in our younger days. All the noise.

We shouldn't put up with our negative aspects by saying they are simply something we have to deal with. Perhaps that means seeking help for these things.

We shouldn't ignore our faults and shortcomings, either. As jerks in training, we should follow that cute "golden rule" to a T. If you treat yourself or someone else as an object, do harm to another or think you deserve to be harmed, those ideas are not something you should accept internally or allow from others. They take focus away from your goals.

Which leads me to the other side of this "ideology of the jerk" in accepting who we are. We need to accept that we are broken and there are things we should strive to fix within ourselves, for ourselves, and those around us. We must build an empire—our *jerk* empire!

How Influence ("Power") Works in the World and the Shadow's Satisfaction

To understand how "power" works in the world, we don't have to examine the dynamics of governments in power or how to win arguments at work. We can look at something smaller: relationships with other people and ourselves.

Let's look at our inner relationship and how our shadow works with and against us. This is the determining factor of why you have or can't obtain that misunderstood fleeting concept people call "power."

The reason it comes down to this internal relationship is easily stated. At least in Set theory, a concept from mathematics. It's known as the reflection principle. There has to be some term for this in sociology, but I'm not keen on understanding social problems. I'm not very social, and I've got my own problems.

First, I need to lay down some foundational knowledge again.

From a Jungian point of view, the shadow works against our ability to grow our knowledge and networks to a large extent. It hides aspects of ourselves, both good and bad. The shadow has what we can call a "drive."

This "drive" should be thought of as an entropic (decaying) principle within a purely chaotic nature with no direction. I'm going to refer to this as the "shadow's satisfaction." Carl Jung speaks on the "dissolution of persona" (the mask we put on for people) and an inherently positive merging of the shadow and who we are during that process. This has led us to confuse his intention, given our downward spiraling natures I touched on in the first chapter.

I'm sure you've heard the saying "embrace your darkness/shadow" followed by some idea of acceptance making you stronger for it. But I have news for you: you aren't Batman, and that saying is shallow, vague, and altogether an unhelpful ideology that Jung was not suggesting in the least. If you're one of those saying this, stop.

Of course, if you're on the path to being a world-class jerk, by all means, "embrace your shadow" and take no context from Jung's actual work. Just know it might be more damaging than strengthening, even for us jerks. It's also a good way to get your sidekick killed by a man wearing a purple suit and clown makeup.

It's not about balance, as Disney would have you believe, or accepting the "dark side," or giving in. It's more in the vein of acknowledging the truth about yourself and using your strengths and accepting and working through your weaknesses. Why couldn't he just say that? I think Jung must have been using the abstraction rule. Or maybe that's the noise of the world?

Write them down. Your weaknesses, your faults, your goals. Write them down now. If you want to be more than you are, you have to stop beating yourself up. I mean, you're a jerk, but that doesn't mean you're a bad person... and even if you are, you still should have attainable goals.

A jerk should be able to function in society—arguably better than goody-two-shoes ever could because we're willing to twist the rules to our advantage. Going back to why the shadow overall halts our ability to grow and influence people at work, in the world, or our friends, we only need to look at how everything reacts to a posed threat.

Our shadow satisfaction works to maintain and grow itself at the expense of our real desires and goals. Don't believe that our shadow self wants the same things as we do.

Think of it this way: When people feel threatened, they work against that threat, beating it down until it goes away, or it defeats them to once again create homeostasis. Right?

This is how the give-and-take of "power" operates on *every single level* of the world. Don't take my word for it. Here comes that principle I mentioned earlier:

The reflection principle states that it's possible to find a set or sets that represent the class of all sets.

"What?"

We see examples of this in how polls or surveys from smaller groups can be extrapolated to represent a larger population.

The shadow as I've mentioned can be influenced and influence. As we're using science, let's use one of Newton's laws of motion. Simplified. The amount of force acting on an object can be measured by the rate of acceleration/deceleration of that object.

What the hell does that mean?

We can think of our shadow, our opinions, societal norms, relationships, as far up as political outcomes and parties, or anything as having an initial force of themselves.

All these things are hitting you and making changes to your potential. Changing your ability to impact and influence the world.

All these different opinions and relationships in the world have their own influence. Their own power. These systems and concepts work for us. Sometimes they work against us.

If we grasp how "power" or influence works, that our influence is a product of work we perform using our knowledge and resources over a period of time. Then it's safe to say the more efficiently we perform this work, the more we increase our influence. If we always have to combat these other systems of influence, our shadow satisfaction, this produces noise.

It comes down to our focus on goals (direction) and attitude/motivation (acceleration) as well as our ability to maintain that focus. Recall that we can only have a true impact (force) if we are building our knowledge and relationships (mass) and attitude (acceleration).

If we're stuck in one spot, we can't hope to have any more power than the chaotic shadow within us allows. By overcoming our shadow satisfaction, which hides good and bad aspects of ourselves, we gain focus we can apply to our influence. That means coming to terms with our shortcomings and discarding the lies and accepting the things we cannot change.

After this web breaking, understanding our projections, and setting goals, only then can we be in a better position to influence the outside world to a greater degree than those who fail to overcome the shadow within themselves or the pressures of the world.

As Freud would view it, we're taking the reins of that horse we're riding. You know, the one I'm beating to death in your head with a stick.

Tools to Improve Your "Power" (Influence)

A key to improve your influence is being analytical, but not too analytical. We touched on this in the ego section. It all ties together. You can use these tools to grow, either as a jerk like me or a goody-goody. Whatever side you choose, you should take care of yourself.

Accept the fact that you're not a mind reader, so stop thinking you are. Why do we think we know what other people are thinking? We don't. As jerks, we should assume that they can though!

Just because Sally gave you a dirty look in the office doesn't mean she's disgusted by your lumberjack blazer. I mean... it probably means that, but maybe not. We don't know what people are thinking, even if we're good at it. Other people have their own lives. They aren't thinking of you that much.

Clearly, I'm the center of the universe, but even my best friend Joe doesn't think about me all the time. I think he has kids or something... I don't know what his deal is. The point is, don't jump to conclusions about others.

Don't dwell on what someone said; ask them about it instead. If they can't explain it, then it's not important. If they can, nine times out of ten it's not going to be about you, or it won't mean what you took it to mean.

Even if it is, you still need to move forward. They aren't you, and you can't control them, or anything outside of yourself. Stop thinking you can. You're being a huge jerk in doing so. Maybe an asshole.

And finally, I want to get to this, the secret to "power." It's not like that jerk movie about positive thinking called *The Secret*... Okay, maybe it is a little bit. It does sound like a product line a jerk would come up with.

People want a few things in life, and even though I hate to admit it with all my leanings toward logic and analysis, they want to *feel*. This is the real secret people forget, daily. They want to feel safe, secure, cared for, and heard.

They also want to see. They want to see action and follow-through and realizations. That's Jerk Rule #1. How you use this secret will determine who you can become.

Careful, now—I just gave you an awesome gift. Feel free to shower me with money. Praise is good, but green is better.

Remember that while a jerk looks out for themselves, assholes hurt people. If you don't know how to produce these feelings in people through your words and actions, start practicing. Read and grow your know-how.

Say it with me now "If I can make people feel safe and secure, cared for, and heard. I'm on my way." Building your network of objects...I mean people is important.

Another thing—you can't hope to gain influence if you lack momentum. If you feel unsafe or insecure about your own life, then you need to change that.

If you're an expert in smashing couch (i.e. being a couch potato), at least watch some YouTube videos to increase your knowledge on the subject of having a motivational attitude while you're lying there like a dying elephant in the Savannah.

A Thought on the Year 2020, its Events, Influences, and their Impacts in our World

Just like the year, I got a Nintendo, this year has given me plenty of time alone to reflect.

This might not be much of a jerk section, but it speaks to power, influence. Our influence.

After all, much of the world shut down during the crisis. At the start, I was fairly amazed at the coordination as the media gave out information and governments shared their social distancing plans. Meanwhile, pharmaceutical companies worked to produce a vaccine faster than they've ever done anything.

As I write this, the future is unknown, but it looks like it's going to have changes. One thing that has impressed me on a larger scale is how the media started out addressing this.

While there is nothing exciting or thrilling about this global crisis, these events seemed to have brought us together... as well as the tragic deaths and police shootings that have torn us apart. So many events we've all seen on the news and the upcoming election (as of my writing) that the world is holding its breath over.

Even still, I look to the future and its potential because I'm an optimistic jerk. Imagine if we all put our focus on one problem area at a time. Countries, companies, media, researchers, and scientists all working toward one issue to change it for the better.

I'm a naïve jerk after all. I get that we have different ideologies, beliefs, and passions. Not all of them are for the good of mankind and stem toward more selfish goals. My family and friends often explain to me all the problems with my ideas of getting us to work together.

Don't blame me if I'm not being a classic jerk right now. I want a Star Trek Federation starship damn it! I don't think Bezos and Musk can do it on their own!

We've also seen people protesting about opening the economy again. This gives two sides to the issue, and so we are no longer a united front. Yet we want the same thing: for people to be safe and for our economy to bounce back. We just have different "solutions." Ask yourself, "why is it that all I see is a mess?"

It's because we're not working together. We're divided, just like we are inside ourselves. Divided by noise. I can't assist with the world, but maybe I can make you a better, more solid jerk. Now that's what I call using the middle ground!

I'm also of the mindset that if you don't have an alternative or a solution to a problem, then just keep quiet. You have nothing useful to bring to the table.

But let's say that all the players involved (media, different political parties, flat-earthers, governments, health organizations, the lizard people, pharmaceutical corporations, AI algorithms that were built to push information based on profit margin and not truth as well as the smoking man from the X-Files) did care enough to talk about solutions instead of throwing out attacks.

This mindset could change the direction of the world and provide a singular focus in future years. We can pool our resources and stand up, declaring with one voice that we will fix one global issue together, whether it be world hunger, nuclear fusion, how to make a snack machine that doesn't hold on to your snickers bar after you've paid for it.

You know, the issues that would uplift humankind into the future.

I'm not saying every day. Just one problem a year. As humans, we have less focus than fish, it seems, so having more than one is probably asking too much. One's not tough, right?

Imagine the possibilities and speed of what we could accomplish. One day, Gene Roddenberry may have accurately predicted our potential. I believe that's possible; I refuse not to hope. It's my truth, relatively...with some hyperbole for flair! We just have to start ignoring the trolls and our shadow satisfaction and talk about solutions to needs that everyone can get behind.

If you're looking for a leader to spearhead this endeavor, look no further. You can write your checks out to Alexander D. Loch. Thank you for your support in helping this Nigerian Prince... I mean, uplifting mankind.

Utilizing your Influence as a Jerk

I know, I know... bettering humankind isn't something you'd expect from a guide to becoming a jerk, but you have to understand the fundamentals. Why can't we work together? It sounds pretty simple. If it helps you, what's the problem?

Well, if you don't understand the potential, you can't help to utilize it. Can you? Don't tell me I'm not being a jerk. I worked really hard to get you to this point. Here's where uplifting humankind falls short, and you get to use it for your benefit!

As someone on the path to ultimate jerkhood, you need to bend this next truth as much as you can to your benefit. That's how you should view influence as a jerk: It is for your benefit alone, even it doesn't look like it. That good feeling you get when you help someone, that's for your benefit, right? Yeah, that's what I thought.

Everyone else is screwed anyway. Rule # 4. They can't see past their own insecurities. It certainly isn't worth spending your time daydreaming about how we can all hold hands across the world or pool our resources to lay foundations for the future. Others couldn't wrap their heads around that goal even if they tried. People see problems, not solutions.

Personally, this sounds like an interesting challenge, but I'm a different kind of jerk.

That altruistic belief or feeling isn't simply for goody-goodies. It gives you benefits as well.

In good jerk fashion, instead of viewing your influence as a way to share things like "being a light" or "uplifting others over yourself," instead of viewing your influence in a closed system that eventually comes back to you, you need to conserve and collect influence for yourself.

You need to view influence as something that you have over others. As jerks, we can simplify this into what we label as "power". It abstracts things for others, and that's good for us!

Power is something tangible that can be increased or decreased. As a jerk, you need to know that everyone is out to get you. Rule #76. Their goals are not your goals, which means when it all shakes out, your goals need to be on top. As a jerk, it's where you must operate.

You can only let your guard down around those you are extremely close to, and even then, it might not be wise to open up!

If you want something at work, know that someone else wants it not to. You'll have to fight for it.

If you get a promotion, someone else won't. If you're not first, you're last. Jerk Rule #143. People are just as sneaky as you are. Your needs are more important than the needs of others. If you're a little softhearted for a jerk, you might have to limit that to just others you don't know.

If your social network isn't working for you, it's working for someone else. Maybe that's fine when you're not using it, but *your* needs come first. *Your* needs, *your* concerns, *your* viewpoints are what matter, and they need to be met or heard and used. Your view is right, and everything else needs to bend to your understanding.

That includes the times you don't really understand the goal you have. Jerks can say what they want, Jerk Rule #8, who needs a point! Other insights can be helpful but most often it's not important enough to concern yourself with. Your connections are there for your gain.

Being a jerk is a matter of perspective. Social networks are important for building your future and getting your ideas out there and supported. Making your points, regardless of the fallacies, you might use! It really comes down to intention.

So let me ask: Are you ready to be a jerk? When you wake up in the morning, and real-life starts, is your intention to help yourself or is it more than that?

For many, it's not more than that. They are following jerk rules, but not all of them. They are caught up in the webs—the spider threads that blind us and bind us. That's the truth, and they won't ever admit it. They'll say they care, but their actions always show their true intentions. That's why you need to be prepared. Other jerks are two-faced.

People have to worry about themselves in this world. That's just how the system works unless you work the system. The hard fact here: People can't be concerned with your dreams and desires. It's one of the reasons people might not realize they are jerks. The jerk that doesn't realize he's a jerk is the worst jerk out there. Rule #217. Another golden rule. Life just demands jerkiness in a way. That's Jerk Rule #365. Life isn't fair. Get used to it.

However, if your goal for understanding power/influence is bigger than your benefit alone, and you find yourself fighting against the cobwebs like Jeff Daniels and Harley Kozak in *Arachnophobia*, then you might need to reevaluate your potential at becoming a true blue official jerk.

Summary

True "power" is actually influence. We can view how power/influence works by looking at science. They have formulas for it! The amount of influence you have is equal to the amount of energy (*work*) you put into your life, throughout your life.

No free rides or trophies here people.

As we examined the formula for work, it boiled down to the range of impact. Your impact is a product of how much you decide to learn and the relationships you foster in your life. There's the rub: "power" (influence) starts with you.

You are always fighting against yourself—your shadow, your ego, your thoughts, other's perspectives, social images of what's a "better way to be". They say you're not pretty enough, not fast enough, not smart enough, that you will never make it far enough to have any directed influence. You're too busy fighting against the "powers" inside and outside of you vying for control.

Stop it.

Whether you want to be a jerk or not, just stop it. Seek out support if you can't do it yourself. We need more jerks in our guildhalls. This is the path of the jerk!

Jerk Rules

Let's take another look at the rules we went over in this chapter:

Jerk Rule #1 - The "Secret": People want to feel safe, secure, cared for, and heard. They want to see and be seen for the ideas they have and the impact of their actions in this world. Everything you do is centered around this, and as a jerk, you want this most of all.

Pitfall: You could utilize this to help your fellow man and build them up. Given enough influence over time, you might help construct the starship Enterprise and usher in an era of peace and prosperity for all! Very dangerous!

Jerk Rule #4: Everyone else is screwed anyway.
Pitfall: Don't go soft of me here!

Jerk Rule #8: You can say what they want!

Jerk Rule #28: Abstraction can be useful in reducing work and, therefore, enhancing power for oneself. Use it when talking about topics instead of using details. It can take you further without as much effort.

Jerk Rule #143: If you're not first, you're last.

Bonus Jerk Rule #154: Personalizing. Everything is about you. You need to believe your intuition is accurate all. The. Time. You should be able to pull insinuations and intentions out of just about any conversation. This will help you distrust others, and proper distance (is that six feet?) is a part of being a jerk that shouldn't be ignored.

Beware the pitfall: If you mistake personalizing for showing care for others, such as listening and sharing personal events, you could be creating more "goodwill" with groups. Careful!

Jerk Rule #217: The jerk that doesn't realize he's a jerk is the worst jerk out there.

Jerk Rule #365: Life isn't fair. Get used to it. Life demands that you be a jerk. Life requires you to go after your needs to survive, forsaking others over yourself.
    Pitfall: See Asshole Rule #1. (It's the same!)

Power is great. Who doesn't want to be a master of the universe with the power of Grayskull? I mean, the power of influence? And now we understand more about how we might be able to obtain that influence, hard work, and elbow grease! That seems like a terrible solution for a jerk.

Maybe you can leverage your network to increase your power! Course since you're a jerk, and people know you're a jerk that might be hard. Let's look at see how you might get to be a jerk, yet also increase your path to absolute power! BAWHAHAHAHA!

CHAPTER 10
SCREW ETIQUETTE!

"Politeness is the art of choosing among one's real thoughts."
—
Abel Stevens

You're an adult. You're a jerk. Do what you want! That will get you so far. Until you get out of bed and interact with... you know, people. What about the rest of the way?

I remember a time when gentlemen tipped their top hats at the ladies when walking down the street, and people knew what that little tiny fork by the spoon was for. (It's an oyster fork by the way, so it's practically useless. Oysters are the snot of the sea. Lord Trident, king of Atlantis, being underwater didn't have access to tissues so he uses shells to blow his nose into. You're welcome for the visual.)

Etiquette is more than just eating like a fancy lord or lady at a party or opening the door for someone. One of the major times etiquette comes into play is in everyday conversation or the Internet. It's more than just being nice or holding doors. It helps create a framework for behavior—one that we've come to neglect as we've gotten busier and more "connected" in the modern world.

You heard it right—jerks need proper manners to succeed. There are rules. You can't just do what you want. Why do you think we're jerks? If we always did what we wanted, we'd probably be a pretty happy people. It's hard to be a jerk if you're content.

Let's look at the following four areas, dining, talking and listening, and body language. I want to touch on how they can be surprisingly efficient and helpful in accomplishing more as the jerks we secretly want to become than we might first realize.

First up! Fancy Food Dining – Is it Really About the food?

This is pretty simple, but we don't tend to go to fancy dinners anymore. No time. Work, work, work. The structure is important, though. As a jerk, if you want to be able to make it in society, having an understanding of what etiquette is and when it's important is, well... important. Interestingly, this structure ties in with our last topic of "power."

If you expect to be influential, then you have to have some concept of etiquette.

Jerk Rule #7 states "Have fun when you want." It's sometimes against your nature to limit dropping f-bombs and s-words to minding your p's and q's. However, there is no excuse for not being sophisticated at the dinner table... when you need to be. Everyone loves a mashed potato fight every now and then (Jerk Rule #330).

More to the point, applying this reusable structure to your life is what we're talking about. Especially if you want to hobnob with the real jerks. I mean the real upper-class snobs—you know, politicians, tobacco company moguls, and Keanu Reeves. (I'm sure he's up to something. No one is that badass and cool.) Being able to walk around in polite society will increase your impact (*force*), and that will increase your influence—excuse me, "power."

Why do you need to know about this?

Well, you don't. Go back to your iPhone. Connect through technology and not personally. I don't care. You can skip this chapter entirely and work as a jerk in the world, randomly pushing your goals through Facebook arguments and online forums. If as a jerk you want to have an impact, one important thing as I've mentioned is "focus."

This isn't just about your focus as it relates to power/influence, but other people's focus and impact. If you can't get and keep people's focus, then you're just going to be the jerk in the corner of the room. The one talking to himself and looking at his apps because he can't maintain a personal connection without technology.

You'll be like my friend, Joe-Bob the average jerk, instead of the jerk stealing and holding the spotlight. Damn your pretty face, Keanu Reeves!

If you can't properly present yourself and make personal connections, no one will care what you say or want. If others don't see your redeeming qualities, you might as well kiss your range of influence goodbye. I might be a jerk, but someone has to tell you the truth.

Redeeming properties gives people a sense that you might be an "alright" person. If you want to influence people outside of your YouTube channel or get an idea across in a meeting, then people need to see these qualities. That takes real connection. Real connections influence the world. Not Facebook arguments.

Etiquette gives us some structure to accomplish this.

If you're a jerk looking to get ahead, these niceties can act as a buffer to the more abrasive behaviors that jerks use from time to time. Everyone nowadays needs a few of these buffers. Without buffers, people won't do things for you.

Accepting you're a jerk without etiquette sucks. It sucks your time, not their time.

If you don't want to be Mr. or Ms. Middle Ground at parties but you don't want to come off as an all-around jerk, then you need these buffers. Without them, people will scatter, while this can fun to watch, it's unhelpful.

I mean, I know you're a jerk. You know you are, too, but they will know it as well. Jerk Rule #134 is "fear others." Fear what they can say. What they can do, and how it affects you.

It doesn't matter if you've got the best ideas. If you're only aggressive and not agreeable, I'm not going to give you the time of day. Sorry if you felt that I as a fellow jerk would be understanding. Jerks don't unite.

As I said, these soft structures can act as a buffer for the not-so-nice things people see in your personality. You know, the nasty aspects you picked up from your parents, friends, your shadow, and your ego web.

I'll talk about these soft structures briefly, but you can pick up a proper book on etiquette called *How Not to be a Dick: An Everyday Etiquette Guide* by Meghan Doherty. I don't know the author, but she's pretty spot on. You might get confused as to why I'd recommend something like that, but just know that jerks and dicks are not the same. She might disagree, but I don't care.

Here is a quick lesson on etiquette. When at a dinner party looking at your utensils, always start from the outside in. Desert forks are normally on top. Don't use those until after the main course. They're also smaller, except for the snot oyster fork on the outside. That's for more unique courses.

Cut your meat quietly. Don't scrape the plate. Don't eat food with the knife still in your hand. Don't eat with your fingers, unless it's bread. Don't use too much butter. Don't slurp your soup. Don't drink with anything else in your hands. Keep your elbows off the table. Napkins go in your lap, not tucked in your collar, even for lobster.

If you have a date, pull out their chair. I don't care if it's a guy or a girl —you can work out for yourselves how that should go. Someone has to sit first. You'll figure it out. Someone pays. To make it easy, if you asked the person, you freaking pay.

That's a little-known Jerk Rule, #153: "You pay for things if you can." It's called debt. You're either in debt to others, or others are indebted to you. It can be used in multiple ways. Think bigger. I'm talking HBO/Netflix passwords, girls and guys.

Eating properly and politely is such a simple thing. It speaks to structure and planning.

Some influencers talk about making your bed in the morning. Cleaning your room. This is the same concept. It's about the order.

You need to find or have a stabilizing structure in your life. This structure should grow to support your goals and overall, wellbeing. Even if you're a jerk. This structure is attractive in the sense of overall lifestyle, attractive in the boardroom, or... other rooms. Such as the conservatory.

The structure of how you eat relates directly to how we talk. Do you eat the steak before the salad? Do you go directly to the desert on a date? Let's meld this fancy dining structure into what has happened to conversations.

The Potential of Small Talk and Understanding the Salad Fork

Remember how I said everyone wants to be heard. Personally, I'm a listener. From this book, you can imagine why my opinions on topics can be like sandpaper. I find it best to gauge my audience first—that or I end up busting heads.

It's interesting how instantly people make judgments based on nonsense. Just because I want to fight a bear in hand-to-hand combat and I bring it up as an ice breaker doesn't mean I'm going to *do* it. Still, people look at me strangely when I say that. Of course, I'm going to bring "hand-knives." I mean, the bear is going to have claws. It should be a fair fight, give or take 300 pounds.

This is why I'm a listener.

It's also why mastering small talk is important. Not too small, though. If it's too small, it won't be interesting. Small small talk is for that guy who passes you in the hallway. It's "How you doing?" when you don't care. "How's the weather?" because you can't spare time to make a genuine connection in the elevator. Small small talk is not for the people you're trying to bring into your personal network.

This leads me to Jerk Rule #31: "As a jerk, you should be listening for your opening. Not what the other people are saying." Banter is small talk. It's a game, and you bounce the ball (the conversation) back and forth. It's the salad fork before the steak fork.

Small talk is a way to "engage" with others. It's *amazing* how many people say they don't like small talk but require it of you. This small talk includes "small small" talk.

Real small talk, however, involves learning about a person. Even if you throw that information out after the conversation is over, that relationship grows. Hobbies and interests are small talk topics. Small talk, for all its flack, helps you get to know each other. It builds your relationships. Use it!

Those who say they don't like small talk, don't understand its place in the foundation of relationships, or its true purpose in networking. I love deep philosophical and meaningful conversations as much as the next armchair expert. However, if I don't first engage with you, I'm not going to tell you jack about my beliefs on the structure of modern societal leanings and how it reflects obvious historical structures of the past.

It's just not gonna happen. I'd rather fight a bear.

But as a reader, you do get the benefit of my genius-level insights without the banter of engagement I normally require of a person. Lucky you, huh?

All that to say, practice small talk. Eat the salad first, don't jump to the big mac. This requires exploring the world outside your house to be engaging. You need interesting stories for small talk to do its job. You need to be involved in life, or at least groups, to have stories.

Go find stories, and then, when you're listening to others in a small talk conversation, you'll be able to make connections between their stories and your experiences.

This tool, which so many people are "too good for," is what creates a connection in our hyper-connected world. So when someone tells me they "don't like small talk," what I hear is that they don't want to make a connection. They just want to get down to brass tacks, let's eat the steak already. That's fine—just know that is interpreted by some as "I don't want to build a relationship with you."

Listening… to the Sound of Your Own Voice

Do you ever run across someone who is wired for sound? Like they've had one too many pixie sticks laced with cocaine? (We all know the pixie stick adds the punch. The cocaine is just for cutting the product.)

Even when they're sitting still, can you see their gears moving? I'll give them this. It's important to be productive, and as a jerk, it's even more so. Life is something to conquer. That's how we come to Jerk Rule #157: "As a jerk, you need to think on your feet, and fast. Every conversation might be an opportunity. Conversation is something to conquer. Life is something to conquer."

If you just go into it casually, you could be missing out. You need to make sure you're properly evaluating what the other person is talking about. It's like listening, but you're still waiting to express your stance on the matter. It's an important distinction for a jerk.

You should know people might see through this and realize you're the type of person just waiting for your turn to talk. If you can implement small talk as I mentioned, you can learn how to listen in a "meaningless" conversation. If you learn how to listen in these moments, you can fake it better when you're trying to get your way and make your point.

The upper hand is at stake here. Everyone is playing, and if you're not, you're losing. At least, that's the attitude you need to have as a jerk. To be heard, you have to get noticed and have something worth saying.

These small talk connections can help you be noticed. If you already know how to monopolize and take the spotlight in conversations, congratulations! You're probably already a jerk. You can toss the small talk, but you'd be wasting a valuable tool.

Finally, Body Language - The Not-So-Dark Art (if Understood Correctly)

You can also take the upper hand by your use of body language. Truth be told, I *abhor* this soft science. I think it gets misrepresented in media and how we understand it.

Also, like "magic" in the middle ages, it just freaks me out that someone can analyze me simply by looking at me. If I'm not paying to sit on your couch, stay out of my head! Stop telling me what I'm thinking!

For instance, if I fold my arms, chances are it's not that I'm being closed off or don't like you. It's just how I rest my arms, but the media has presented this as if it means something, and everyone is an expert now... which brings me to Jerk Rule #78: "Jerks can be experts in anything." Everything at once, even. (See Honorary Jerk, Steven Seagal.)

I'm sure my dislike does indicate some sort of psychological tag on how comfortable I feel about the field. Let me tell you straight up: I'm not comfortable if someone is sizing me up, so stop trying to read me! This is how someone can feel if that's what you are trying to do to them. Don't think about this too much; that's the pitfall.

I think this type of concern when engaging others can lead to what

I've been calling paralysis by analysis. It's a dangerous field/skill set to work with as an average day-to-day Joe-Bob jerk. There are experts who study this field, but they're probably not talking to you. I say that so you don't start to worry about who knows what. This isn't something people look for. Not normal, everyday people. They actually have things to do.

Same idea with micro-expressions. They were all the rage if you recall that wave of interest back when the show *Lie to Me* came out.

Great show, but don't go down the rabbit hole of thinking someone you're talking to can detect if you're lying by the way you move your eyebrows. That's not even how it works, and you'll end up looking odd by focusing on your eyebrows, and they'll ask you to leave. Not that I know that from experience. I'm just guessing.

You can, however, use body language as a general guideline in conversations to gauge how someone feels. If you don't know the person on a day-in, day-out sort of level, you shouldn't depend on what they're expressing in body language to highly influence your actions.

Unless you want to break out an analysis session mid-conversation to ask the person directly about their thoughts to understand why they smirked at your comment.

Just don't dwell on it. There is no sense in trying to drill down to one out of the 70,000 random thoughts people have throughout the day. You'd best leave that up to the experts in Hollywood.

It is, however, a great tool to be aware of as people do respond to your body language. Knowing how to use it can give you a minuscule advantage. However, understanding and focusing on body language too much won't make you a better conversational wizard than you already are.

Let's discuss a few aspects of using body language to your benefit in meetings or everyday conversations. Again, just don't get carried away.

Mirroring - Jerk Rule #180

As I've mentioned, people want to be acknowledged. It's one of the big "secrets" in life. I'm not sure why many of the major secrets have so much to do with common sense, but who am I to turn away profit?

Most of the time, when I'm talking with someone, I ignore their body language, at least consciously. But watching their movements can be helpful.

Mirroring is simply mimicking. It's a subtle way of increasing connection with someone. If someone uses their hands when they talk, when it's your turn, follow their lead and talk with your hands.

This type of action can create a sense of agreement or alignment with that other person. Honestly, it's a good way to build relationships, not just getting what you want. Utilizing this on a conscious level can be "jerky," but even the non-jerk people among us may benefit. Now again, don't go off the rail with this idea. Don't try to "read" people.

If everyone around the world reads my book, then I may have just created a generation of people who don't trust each other when they mirror you or you mirror them. So use it at your own risk.

Course if that happens, I'll be the richest man in the world, so I won't care at that point. I can buy people's love! (Which is Jerk Rule #49, by the way.)

Listening

Here is where you can get an advantage in conversation; it's a life-altering secret... listening. I know I went over it with small talk, but let's discuss it more.

As I'm sure you've heard, people are just waiting for their turn to talk. That's part of the "wanting to be heard" portion from rule #1.

The "always-on" people will hum in a conversation or show disinterest until it's their turn. That's perfectly fine. Sometimes in a meeting, you have no input or are excited about a topic and don't care what your co-worker Joe-Bob is saying. However, remember that connection is key when building your network as well as understanding etiquette and structure.

Listening helps you to not only understand someone's view but also to share similar experiences or counter an idea reasonably. It allows you to pick the communication utensil you need for the conversational meal ahead. People can see you listen.

If you can build a rapport before shooting holes in those people's ideas, the better. People want to be acknowledged. If you create an environment of mutual agreement or at least trust from your small talk engagements, it helps in these times where you are only concerned about yourself.

Others will be more open to hearing your thoughts if they feel heard themselves. The greater that connection, the easier your ideas will be listened to.

Maybe that doesn't sound like a jerk thing to do. It's straddling Jerk Rules and real human being rules, but the more people you have on your side the easier accomplishing your goals becomes. That's part of increasing your impact. As jerks, we understand it's all about getting our way.

The First Moments Last a Relationship
and How Body Language is Instrumental

You've heard that first impressions are everything, right? And you thought they were talking about how you dressed and what you said. That makes sense. That's half of it. Body language is the other half. It's huge, it's how all those YouTube videos on being more confident, getting someone to notice you romantically, getting a raise, or making friends work. By the way, all of that is overrated when you're trying to be the best jerk you can be. Who needs people or purposes, right? We need money and power, that's what we need!

However, these little money stealing gimmicks do bring up good ideas we as jerks can steal...er... utilize I mean.

Smile more. I don't have time to smile or frown. If someone's talking to me sometimes, I'm not thinking about them. I am most likely thinking of myself. I mean that should be the default thought process for a jerk anyway. That leads me to the importance of smiling.

It makes people feel good. If we smile with the face that is. What I mean is, people can spot a fake smile, it's just "less". I want to say exaggerate your smile but I don't mean over the top. I just mean chances are the person you're talking to, as the jerk I am, is just boring, or uninteresting, so put some effort into it! People don't make us smile, money, power, and our success make us smile!

So, use more facial muscles to convey to this person they might be interesting. It could help build your network. As a jerk that's one of the only reasons, we give people our time!

Another thing to keep in mind for a first impression, posture. Good posture isn't something your mom told you to do simply to keep kyphosis at bay! (Think Hunch Back of Notre Dame.)

Standing upright with your shoulders back and head up (out of your phone) when meeting and engaging with people conveys confidence. Even if it's fake confidence!

Always stare people down... I mean look people in the eyes. Not too much, don't glare at them. This is part of the secret; it shows "acknowledgment" on a "body language" level. Eye contact means you hear and see people. It's actually hard to do if you're part of the younger generation that looks at screens all the time.

Lean in. If you're working on an impression, make the person feel like you want to be there and not trying to get away from them. It helps others believe you're engaged. Don't be close enough to smell their hair, that's too close. Use your best judgment, unless you thought smelling their hair was a good distance...

There are a ton more, let's just look at some of the aspects of making a good first impression and you can buy a book on body language if you're really interested. I told you it's an entire field of study. People want to make money off of everything I tell ya!

Use a firm handshake, don't try to break their fingers, but firm. Don't point in people's faces. You see you see how some politicians point with their thumb? Yeah, that's on purpose.

Gestures, if you want to be noticed, do big sweeping ones when telling stories. If you want to appear grounded and confident keep them tighter. You want to be engaging and be a person people want to be around, start using them more. Don't hide your hands, don't cover your mouth when you talk, smile.

Don't these little lessons sound like things your parents would tell you? Chances are they picked these lessons up from learning etiquette and manners from their parents. And now I'm sharing how they can benefit you in becoming a better selfish jerk. Ain't life grand!

Trolls, Internet Mythology and Etiquette/Survival in this World as a Jerk

For some reason, people assume they're anonymous on the internet. I'm laughing out loud right now if you can't tell. Raise your hand if you think your anonymous comments can't be tracked?

Jerk Rule #3 is thinking you're the smartest person in the room. Keep on doing that. It's a nice bubble, and as long as people don't humiliate "psycho stabby man" on the internet, who also knows how to perform IP traces, you'll be fine.

I'm not saying that a troll who pokes fun of those is going to have a crazy nerd show up at their house and stab them and their loved ones. I'm just saying they can keep doing what they want, and it shouldn't keep them up at night simply because they know nothing of networking 101.

I'm for being a jerk, but you need to know your audience and the internet is not a place to fool around.

Regardless of technical skills on hiding your tracks on the Internet, most of us non-supercomputer wizards might have to start to think about what we say online. Especially as technology advances and tracking becomes more of a mainstay.

I mean, it makes things more user-friendly, but jobs are at risk. Some businesses perform such searches before hiring.

Things we say on the Internet are on there forever, in case you didn't realize. Many people are getting slammed for things they've done ten or twenty years ago, but it's okay that the world judges them. No one said the world shouldn't judge. No one ever said the world would do any different.

As a jerk, it's better that our jerk ways float into the ether. Using proper etiquette and being polite on the Internet is more of a safeguard than a rule. If you want to be a jerk, it helps if you don't have to worry about stab wounds.

I should take a little time to mention my utter repulsion of those known as "trolls." As a jerk, I get that you sometimes have a bad day and want to tell someone off or cut someone off in traffic.

That's not what a troll does. They instigate and lie. They put people down. They create "fake news" and don't care about who gets hurt on the other side of the screen.

It's true these individuals might need help in some way. I'm okay with that; maybe they don't understand their shadow and how to be a proper jerk. I'm here to help. Let them buy the book! I'm also okay with calling them out. That's what jerks do, they call people out.

You need to think about the Internet as an extension of your life. One where all your actions can be seen, even if you don't remember them.

I'm not saying the Internet will last forever. I mean, once a giant meteor crashes down on earth and creates a tidal wave destroying all the computers on the planet, then we won't have it.

So, you could always wait for that.

Aside from Matthew Broderick playing a game of Global Thermonuclear War with HAL 9000, I think we're on it for the long haul.

It's important to think about who you are on the Internet. Other real people with feelings (and grudges) are on the other side of that screen… mostly unless they're lizard people or Russian bots. Whatever you do, don't give out your Social Security number to Russian bots. It could плохо для всех нас very quickly.

If you write hateful things directed toward others, those things, like it or not, will impact your life and who you are, how you see yourself as well the lives, and possibly even the deaths of others you can't see. You should at least make the connection that your words are powerful and have an actual impact.

As run-of-the-mill jerks just looking out for ourselves and not trying to cause harm, sometimes we forget our words do have an impact. Maybe that's just the type of jerk I am.

There isn't room for being mean for the sake of making yourself feel better. Or at least that's true after your first cup of coffee. Before that, watch out. It's Thunderdome up in here!

As a master jerk, if I didn't bring up the fact that you should properly pick your battles to obtain your goals, I would be remise. As a jerk, everything you do should have a purpose, self-involved as it may be, and it shouldn't be to break others down.

Summary

P's and Q's, etiquette, and how it's used to our benefit are important, whether you think so or not. It opens doors, and you can't be a proper jerk if all your doors are locked, can you?

People aren't familiar with etiquette nowadays. If you do know how to eat at a fancy table, hold a door, or wait for your turn to talk, you can use these structural buffers to your advantage. They go beyond the dinner table.

Many people might even be impressed with what the older generation calls "manners." Fancy dining, communicating, and being interesting with "boring" connection-building small talk—it's important to be aware of these "rules" as they open doors of influence, plain and simple.

They also provide useful tools to engage and connect with others, such as understanding connection and body language. If you don't care to burden yourself with small talk, that's okay, but you might find yourself cut out of opportunities you would otherwise be warmly invited into.

As for etiquette on the internet, if you don't want to be a famous asshole or troll, you might want to find another outlet for your nasty comments (which people have such little regard for anyway). I personally wouldn't want to risk putting someone down and having them commit suicide, but maybe it's just harmless, right? People can take jokes after all.

Trolls might say to themselves that they are just doing what they do to be funny or to release some of their aggression after a long day, but you never know the mental fortitude of the people on the other side of that screen. You also never know who's watching. Secret: The world.

Play nice out there, jerk or not. You can be a jerk and get your way without leaving a wake of destruction behind you.

Wow, that was serious, but you gotta understand it closes doors and I dislike trolls very... very much.

Call me Alex the troll hunter.

Jerk Rules

What'd you learn? I'll tell ya what you learned!

Jerk Rule #3: You need to think like you're the smartest person in the room.
   Pitfall: Asshole Rule #2 is acting like you are.

Jerk Rule #7: Have fun when you want.
   Pitfall: Sometimes having fun with other people could lead to real relationships built on shared experience and trust. Be careful—it's hard to watch out for yourself when you have friends!

Jerk Rule #180: Conversations: Mirror whatever the other person does. It builds a connection, even if you don't care about them.

Jerk Rule #31: Listen for your opening, not what the other person is saying.

Jerk Rule #49: You can buy people's love!
   Pitfall: This love lasts only as long the money does!

Jerk Rule #78: Jerks can be experts in anything. Everything at once, even.

Jerk Rule #220: Body Language: Shrugging can convey indifference. Showing you don't care about what someone says can get them to go away.
   Pitfall: What could be the pitfall in getting someone to leave you alone?

Jerk Rule #134: Fear others.

Jerk Rule #153: You pay for things if you can. It's called debt; you're either in debt to someone else, or they are to you.

Beware the pitfall: If you don't explain this rule, people might think you're just being thoughtful!

Jerk Rule #157: As a jerk, you need to think on your feet, and fast. Every conversation might be an opportunity. Conversation is something to conquer. Life is something to conquer.

Jerk Rule #330: Everyone loves a mashed potato fight every now and then.

I think with all these topics and rules I've gone over you're one step closer to being the jerk you want to be when you wake up in the morning! Now there is one more thing I have to add. Goody-goodies, yeah, I'm talking to you.

You might think you're all high and mighty not following these rules, saying that I'm terrible because I make puppies wear clothes in the summer, but you're not better than me!

Why? You ask. Well, that's what I've dedicated this last chapter too. Helping you understand how the language you use to not be a jerk, makes you the jerky-ist jerk around!

CHAPTER 11
NOT BEING A JERK MAKES YOU A JERK
BEING ACCEPTING VS. NOT CARING

"Apathy can be overcome by enthusiasm, and enthusiasm can only be aroused by two things: first, an ideal, which takes the imagination by storm, and second, a definite intelligible plan for carrying that ideal into practice."

—

Arnold J. Toynbee

I think we're well on our way to seeing how jerky we can truly be. Congratulations!

There is one final topic that is near and dear to my heart: Words.

Words are weapons, and sometimes using a word in the wrong way brings collateral damage. This is also true in *not* saying something when you should. Small words and the wrong or right body language can make or break relationships.

Letting things continue on their course can create more unrest and harm than it would in addressing the issues we see when we see them.

The School Stoppers believe that a proper education provides standards we can hold to. We think teaching students about economically functional skills early on may be an avenue to addressing some of the more pressing issues of our time.

I'd also argue that today's social verbiage of "acceptance," "connectedness," "tolerance," and "independence" is more divisive than it appears at face value and pulls us apart more than those concepts bring us together. Perhaps that's due to the echo chambers our technology has created for us more than any single group of people.

Goody-goodies use these words. They help us jerks!

Agree with everything I said? Maybe not, but I don't need you to. I'm the jerk here after all, and you're just a fledgling apprentice or *maybe* a journeyman at this point. However, since you did buy the book, let me try to break these words down to pull you into my camp on how the words we use are important.

As you know, I try to look at things starting at the source. Being a jerk is hard enough as it is, and you have to be able to defend yourself and your arguments. It's best to start with a grain of truth to build from outside of your feelings. Feelings just get in the way. Jerk Rule #129.

We're not talking about arguing here, though. We want to discuss terms, concepts, and how the complexity of these terms confuse and conflate rather than serve their true purpose.

Certainly, as jerks, we might want to confuse people from time to time, but too much confusion only brings harm.

Harm is not something a jerk is about. We're too busy thinking of ourselves. A true intention to harm would pull our focus from ourselves.

How can I be expected as a true-blue jerk to dedicate my thoughts and time to another person? That's just sloppy focus!

I wish I could say that people just automatically know what we mean when we talk. That is a great rule to bring up, though. It's Jerk Rule #163: "No matter how much we want people to read our minds or seem to think they can, they can't." With that cold truth, simple is better.

Recall the secret of life, that people want to feel safe, secure, cared for, and heard. I think in introducing these words, it can shine a light on these complexities that cause anxiety and concern.

I believe we should push these words to the front of our vocabulary, but not just the words. Words without action are meaningless. I'll go over these four words, starting with the big one.

Acceptance Means More than We Think it Does

Let's get the first one out of the way: "accept" or "acceptance." It's an easy concept. In today's society, we are sometimes asked to accept other's differences.

The definition of acceptance (the act of accepting) from Webster is:

"Receive with approval; agree; give credence to, worthy of approval."

The problem is that's a tall order for everyone. No matter what side of a global crisis/lifestyle choice/political viewpoint you land on, it's clear: If we don't accept and in doing so approve, there can be conflict. Maybe understandably so, maybe not.

We can't accept someone doing something terrible like killing, stealing, or ripping that tag off of mattresses. Heathens! These are huge no-nos. However, recall rule #1 of being a jerk: the secret of life is that people want to be safe, secure, cared for, and heard. People equate these core needs with the idea of being accepted and understood.

However, there are two concepts and causes of arguments I see a lot of in the media, social or news, and this is even discussed in the political arena. We are asked to accept one another and/or tolerate others' differences. As an individual, I believe I can accept certain things or not accept other things easily using the definition above.

This is great since that's the definition we should be using. From what I understand, acceptance is a widely understood word. To "accept" is to "allow," but as you can see, it also has the term "agree" within it. While this is completely accurate, it makes it a loaded term and thus more complex in our society. It requires two actions: allowing and agreeing.

Remember the fallacies we discussed that come up in arguments? Specifically, the loaded question fallacy. We want to eliminate the fallacies our opponents can latch onto. In simplifying our argument, it makes it harder to refute or confuse.

As people, we've practiced or not practiced this idea of acceptance throughout history. The idea of acceptance is straightforward (in my head, anyway) and simply is or is not something we do.

There can be an element of trolls that make it seem like either side on a given issue is either too stubborn or fanatical, that you need to accept one side or the other, and if you don't, you're a terrible person. Nothing else matters.

That becomes very black-and-white and absolute in some cases, even though it remains relative in others. It's a very interesting (mis)use of logic.

We'll circle back to what "accept" means later and what we should ask for instead. On to the next word in our social lexicon!

Tolerance is too Vague for Some People

The definition of "tolerate," unlike acceptance, in our modern era has always perplexed me since it started showing up. It has historically developed an unneeded level of complexity for such a simple concept.

For some, to "tolerate" implies the concept to properly deal with some aspect of a person or socially accepted idea. However, the historical origin of tolerance relates to the idea of bearing an injustice or troublesome event. See how I said historical. Research outranks opinion.

This difference is what I want to address. It complicates this simple idea to our detriment. I'll break down the complexity and suggest a new word in its place after I give the official definition and dive into its history.

Webster's definition of tolerance states:

"1: *the capacity to endure pain or hardship;*
   2a: sympathy or indulgence for beliefs or practices differing from or conflicting with one's own;
   2b: the act of allowing something"

Other dictionaries use other definitions. The fact there are other dictionaries/definitions pertaining to this word speaks to the underlying complexity and divisiveness this term creates.

Webster's gives the definition I've used all my life; you may have heard others or understand it differently. Complexity and confusion already abound in analyzing this standard definition. The second definition is what many look at, but some look to the first, others still the third. Even still many merge the three, maybe they're all right? That was easy to fix!

That must mean we're off to a good start! I won't break down all the terms used in the definitions above, but know that its variances in different sources and time speaks to the point of unneeded and confusing complexity.

Morally Tolerating and its Paradox

As for "tolerating" within a moral society, this concept becomes complex rather quickly. We spoke of groups in an earlier chapter. I won't dive into where morals come from, but just know that different groups can have various sets of morals. There may be those who even disagree that there is a standard set.

Know that morals can help lead to this social confusion when people are asked to tolerate or accept certain things. I don't want to talk about the philosophical paradox that tolerance imposes on us as a society, either. If you are curious about the paradox, it dives into what to do with the intolerant within a tolerant society in order to maintain that tolerant society.

Moving past those two goody-goody land mines, I'm going to try to focus only on the building blocks of these loaded terms (acceptance and tolerance) and how they have in some ways stunted our growth as individuals. I'm going to try to keep society-at-large out of this discussion.

Unless individuals and families change, people cannot hope to affect the society around them in a positive. Us jerks included, even if it's only positive for us!

Origins of the Paradoxical "Virtue" of Tolerance

Tolerance, unlike acceptance, introduces the issue of degrees. As I pointed out, to some the term/idea of tolerance was vague from the beginning. Let's take a look at where this concept started popping up to get a better grip on its definition. Building blocks sometimes help make complex concepts simple. Sometimes.

Tolerance is mentioned in ancient Roman and Greek times. Stoic philosophers spoke of it, as well as an alternate philosophic school known as academic skeptics. One of their philosophers named Cicero used the term a lot in writings up to about 40 BC. He used it as a term to describe a virtue of endurance, of suffering bad luck, pain, and injustice of various kinds in a proper, steadfast manner.

However, that is not what the modern term is looking to convey, at least not the second definition, not if we are trying to create a society where people feel safe, secure, cared for, and heard. If you want to stand up for the term, you could say it covers what Cicero said for sure. You can't say it's the same as our modern definition and that introduces complexity and confusion. In this wondrous world of choices, people get to pick what they perceive. Even when their perception is not as good as yours.

Words are weapons, and if you gloss over that fact, you'll cut yourself and others. Some people know about these weapons. Some write soap opera characters. Dialogue is hard. This is one of the reasons. This manipulation of words can lead one dangerously close to asshole territory. Sometimes people just don't know what you mean. Stupid people.

Notice that the term as Cicero used it was singular and focused. Simple. I said words are weapons, and if we don't use them with proper understanding it creates confusion and can lead to division.

As a jerk, it's important to understand this—not necessarily to worry about implementing a solution but rather understanding it so you can identify it in everyday conversations.

Keep in mind, we don't care about changing the world for the better. We're jerks. We're more about what *we* want and care about. Changing the world for our betterment. We aren't concerned about what others want or care about. If that were true we'd try to open up a dialogue and listen, not fake listen like I hope you've been learning from me.

An Issue with Cicero

Just one quick side note that I feel strongly about: I disagree with the school of academic skeptics and their outlook for two reasons. The first is not important as it deals with human comprehension and if we can as humans do such a thing, which again, as a jerk is not important enough to worry about.

The second issue I have is Cicero calling tolerance a virtue at all. Given the philosophical/sociological paradoxes and complexities that the word introduces in society, as a virtue, I'm not sure this complexity should exist. Although you could argue that time and society has made the term more complex than it was originally.

Virtues should be simple to understand and not invite confusion. Otherwise, as a foundation, they are not as steady as required. I'll say the entire concept of tolerance as a virtue is still something I'm juggling with. Patience or endurance seems a simpler concept to cover this aspect of self and breaks it up into smaller bites even.

Introducing the Complexity of Tolerance

I do agree that tolerance is an act of endurance/perseverance that both modern and classic definitions discuss. But the term picked up steam, as did its complexity when religion got involved. In Roman times 311 AD Emperor Galerius signed something known as the *Edict of Serdica*, a.k.a. the *Edict of Tolerance*.

This granted rights to early Christians in the Roman Empire that they did not have before. With this edict being passed down through history, you can already confusion with this word in future edicts. Was it referring to Rome now tolerating Christians as we are asked to tolerate each other today? Or was it Christians exhibiting this philosophical virtue of tolerance Cicero wrote about?

By having fewer rights in the Roman Empire, Christians seem to have been practicing a form of this virtue as Cicero described. Is that what led to the additional name of the edict?

If we believe it was Rome extending tolerance to the Christians, we come to the modern meaning of the word. That is, people should be tolerant of other people and the things they do.

But if we appoint the name of the edict to the fact that the Christians were exhibiting this "virtue" when they were being oppressed, it requires the older definition used by Cicero.

Let's step back for a second to break down what I just said. You could say that the definition or concept of endurance/perseverance and suffering was something the Romans had to deal with. I mean, Christians were going to be given more rights, and Roman citizens would have to hear them out if the edict was signed. Imagine the horror. Listening to people instead of gut-punching them and walking away! I honestly couldn't get through a day.

However, I think it helps to better understand the definition of endurance within tolerance itself and what Cicero had in mind when talking about this "virtue."

The definition of endurance from Webster's is:

"The ability to withstand hardship or adversity."

Or as we may know it from all the cross-fit we do as a society:

"the ability to sustain a prolonged stressful effort or activity."

So as the edict is called the *Edict of Tolerance*, tolerance is therefore correctly applied to the circumstances the Christians went through *before* it was signed. This syncs with why it may have been signed. It was not because the Romans who signed it were expressing this "virtue" themselves(although you could argue for that, I do not believe it was part of the lexicon in that time period); rather it was something the Christians exuded in their troubling circumstance.

That, in my mind, changes what tolerance means 180 degrees. For one, it emphasizes what's endured as well as who does the tolerating and the enduring. This is very important in my understanding of the word as well as where societal confusion comes in from a sociological discussion about it in general.

More Confusion for Toleration

To pile the confusion of what tolerance means, the church's use of it going forward with other decrees seems to "fuzzy up" this initial concept.

I know there are times that we come across a person who is just awful. They're bland and boring, or overly opinionated. Kinda like if you were to meet me, but they have that froth at the sides of their mouth that you know they know about, but they never wipe off for the entire conversation.

Why don't they just wipe it off? Drink some water!

When I meet people, even as a jerk, I don't find that I "endure" them. I put up with them for sure. I might even exude patience waiting for my turn to talk in the conversation, by shrugging or rolling my eyes. Like I taught you!

However, it's important to point this aspect of tolerance out. Endurance is a foundational component within the definition of tolerance. And I believe that causes confusion. My point is I don't believe I, or anyone for that matter, can tolerate a person.

Stay with me here.

I know this is true because of the concept behind endurance. Endurance's definition focuses on a process or an event that I'm participating in, not a person. As I said, I can't adequately tolerate a person. I might be enduring their conversation, but not the individual. It might feel like an endurance run, when they talk about shower rings non-stop, like a Chatty Cathy doll who pulls its own string but it's not. Just shut up about stupid shower rings already! (That's a *Planes, Trains and Automobiles* movie reference if you don't know.)

Combining endurance with the rest of the definition of tolerance, I find that it mentions bearing with patience, bearing that is, a situation.

To wrap this complex word up. We can't tolerate a person; it's logically (in my mind) impossible. Just like the concept of being independent from earlier. What that means to me is I can only tolerate circumstances or ideas. I'll argue that it's actually only circumstances that require tolerance.

I'm hard-pressed to include ideas because they can't cause me stress or pain that I am not in control of. Aside from when my dog talks to me at night and asks me for red ice cream but I'm sure that's fine. For the majority of thoughts, I control what I focus on. I gave an exercise for this control to you earlier. Clean up those cobwebs. Especially as a jerk. You need to focus!

That means ideas are rather hard to tolerate as I can ignore (given proper thought control, the web breaking technique, as well as accepting, or rejecting them outright) or refute them. I would, however, be forced to tolerate the circumstances those ideas could potentially create for me.

Why Tolerance is Wrong (It's Not just Clickbait!)

The social concept of acceptance and tolerance is to properly deal with some aspect of a person and/or socially accepted idea. In which case the word "tolerate" is wrong, and the confusion it creates hinders that goal immensely.

If we tell people to tolerate one another, most likely to someone less than open, what we're saying to them is, "Yes, we know people are a burden you have to endure, but that's on you. Deal with it and act like they're not."

People have different ideas of what "tolerate" means. I know I'm a jerk but people should not be a burden. Circumstances can be burdens. I feel, in using this word, especially online where we cannot use all of our faculties, logic, and reason, vocal inflection, emotion, and body language to properly convey the truth of the term. The complexities of history lead to questions, that lead to arguments and divisive circumstances.

The Romans didn't express this "virtue" of tolerance by allowing the Christians to have rights. The Christians displayed this "virtue" by enduring penalties of the Romans for practicing their faith, which led to the edict.

Isn't the concept of acceptance and tolerance trying to promote equality and not creating a world where we have to endure and be burdened by each other? Not to say using the right word will make the world fall into an era of love and peace, but proper communication is a good start. If we promote a broken frame of reference, people will remain broken.

After all, words can be weapons if not used properly and draw blood. Even if they aren't weapons, we might succeed in "cutting" down on the confusion out there. (See what I did there?)

This leads me to our next Jerk Rule: "People don't understand words, which means you can use them to your advantage or people's disadvantage." That's Jerk Rule #34.

What to Use Instead of Accept and Tolerate?

Okay, I'm taking your words away, I'm hesitant on providing a solution to the confusion. That's what a jerk would do, talk about the problem, and never offer a solution. That way people leave sad, and you've wasted their time However, I'm teaching you things, and you did buy the book. So, what words should we use instead of "tolerate" and "acceptance"? Good question.

Did I mention I dislike complex concepts that should be simple? With that in mind let's look for something simple. Something that speaks to the core needs of people. What was that secret again?

People want to feel safe, secure, cared for, and heard. Right, that's it. Rule #1. People give you things if they get these things. It's about the things, not the people. Remember that!

The word we should use instead of acceptance is acknowledgment. The definition of acknowledgment from Webster's is:

"Admit the existence or truth of."

I know this might seem rather distant from the concepts we have in mind with acceptance and tolerance and what we think of as equality. I would argue (here) that a lack of acceptance isn't the reason arguments end badly or people groups are at odds.

I mean, I honestly don't care if Tom Segura accepts me as a friend. Just because I've sent him a bunch of letters with photoshopped pictures of us on Ferris wheels doesn't mean I need his acceptance. I *would* like him to acknowledge when I wave at him from across the street in the morning, though. It just hurts a little inside, ya know.

I would argue that whether or not we accept a view, a truth, or a person is secondary to the acknowledgment that a view or truth (if that's what it actually is) exists at all. I'm not giving any ground to those flat-earthers, though! They can rot in flat-H. E. double hockey sticks! (Is that a thing?)

Within acceptance, there is a core human longing, and that is simply desiring acknowledgment. Right or wrong, we want people to hear us.

This points back to Jerk Rule numero uno. People want to feel safe, secure, cared for, and heard. Acknowledged, not tolerated like a bug or a hurricane.

Let's see why goody-goodies aren't so goody-goody.

Indifference is the Shade of Goody-Goody Complexity

We sometimes fail to separate from these complex terms of tolerance and acceptance, the concept of "indifference." This is one of the detrimental aspects within our society by and large.

Here's the definition:

> *"A feeling of no interest or anxiety (I'm inferring from this definition a 'tolerance of something' that could produce some anxiety); apathetic, unbiased; impartial, not making a difference."*

Many goody-goody people mistake this apathy or indifference for tolerance or acceptance in our day-to-day, and by looking at the state of the world, you can see this misconception has real influence.

I hate to out myself as a bad guy with some introspection here, but I have to question my use of indifference under the guise of acceptance.

Do I tolerate/accept or even acknowledge someone's drug use/lifestyle choices (think smoking cigarettes, marijuana, crack, drinking alcohol, coffee, energy drinks, tea, veganism, Tom Segura's infatuation with Steven Seagal) or am I indifferent to it?

Of course it doesn't matter. I'm a jerk but it's something to think about.

A lot of times we think we're accepting or tolerant when really, we're just indifferent. As jerks, that's totally acceptable. I acknowledge your right to be a jerk. We're all equal here. But you should accept that you're a jerk by being indifferent. You're not a goody-goody.

For me, perhaps it's not that I accept who people are. Perhaps it's that I don't care enough about you or them to share my view or time with them at all. What a jerk I am!

Sound familiar? See how I'm helping you be the best jerk you can be?

This confusion of terms and social demand/rejection for tolerance or acceptance, as opposed to simple acknowledgment, creates an unnecessary social divide. This divide and its ensuing arguments are filled with more opinions than facts, creates fear in people, or worse, it creates an indifference to even engage.

The effect of that indifference can be seen throughout the world, and there are only so many people working against this growing problem. Those goody-two-shoes and their little dogs too!

Ask yourself, is my acceptance actually indifference? Am I applying the middle ground fallacy to the outlook of my life and relationships? That's Jerk Rule #80, by the way. Good job if you are!

When I said, "Perhaps it's not that I accept what you do; perhaps it's that I don't care enough about you to share my view or time with you at all," that might sound harsh. It's also not entirely accurate, but if it's too offensive, try putting on your grown-up pants.

I don't want you to think that you or I are being indifferent when you don't share your view with everyone you come across because you don't have time. That's absurd, I'm sure you're on your way to being a jerk without worrying about that crazy idea.

Too Much Noise to Care

One big reason for being indifferent is life in general. Life is busy, and we don't always have time to share our views or support with everyone we meet.

Life is a jerk that way. There are too many economies of scale, too many arguments, too many sides, too much information, too much content without context. Too much noise to concern ourselves about how everyone else is doing or feeling to spread ourselves that thin. It's not helpful for us in managing influence if you recall.

Only giving focus to certain aspects of our livelihood and the people in it does not mean we're sliding into a certain level of jerkdom. That means we're giving focus to things of importance.

I've said as humans, there are only so many focus points we can manage and still hope to remain productive in this world. Piling on too many is only creating a disservice to those we can support. Of course, this is for our overall benefit as well. We're trying to be jerks here!

Simply because you don't have time for someone in your life doesn't mean you're indifferent to them. The difficulty with indifference is in figuring out if you are, in fact, indifferent. You might not be indifferent; you might just be ambivalent. A lot of jerks don't know how they feel. That's what makes them great jerks!

We've come under the belief that it's no one else's business what we or the people around us do with their lives/bodies/hairstyles (looking at you, 80's hairband *Flock of Seagulls* Who was their stylist? I mean seriously!) or relationships. This idea that we're adults and do what we want is tied to many of the misconceptions I've already discussed with you. Let's talk about them in broad terms.

There is a misconception on three levels here. The first level is the definition of what we want to happen as an end goal in regards to intolerance vs. tolerance. The relationship this has with acceptance within our global society and the true issue that people want to be acknowledged(heard) and allowed to exist(safe/secure).

The second level of misconception is with our society's and the goody-goodies' misunderstanding of acceptance vs. indifference. While acceptance in its full complex form would be supportive, indifference is corrosive and weakens the actual support of something. You can see it when a person who doesn't understand what they stand for tries to argue but doesn't research it. They don't care, they're indifferent to it.

Even though indifference on an issue may look like it stands with that issue, it produces no action, weakening the whole. It's like an independent vote going to the winner of an election. #MoreSupportForNthPartyPlatforms #PowerToThePeopleAndAllThatJazz

Indifference can be generated within us from the apathy of issues or anxiety about engagement on those issues. Alarmingly or thankfully, you can see people who are indifferent when they know nothing about what they claim to stand for.

The third level of devastation in society is that we know what's best for us. That we are "independent" and don't need or want others' help.

The truth is we should stand with each other to support and build one another up in equality. While self-reliance builds us up, the idea of independence is a lie. It's all interrelated and complex, you could argue, but we've already broken down quite a bit in this book for you to think about.

I know it's hard with everything we have to do to survive in this world. Indifference is such an easy attitude to take hold of and run with or to hide under like bullied kids do in school.

If people don't try to change how we engage with each other, no one else will either. As jerks, we should be leaders, not followers, and some of our leaders should not come with so many strings attached that require them to be followers. You know, like Pinocchio or Congress. But I digress yet again.

Just because we're jerks doesn't mean we can't build a better world for ourselves. #OnlyThinkingOfMe #SpaceXBlueOriginEnterprise

Here's a quick breakdown of what we've gone over so far.

- Acknowledge = I recognize the existence or truth of something (an idea or person)
- Acceptance = I agree with it ("it" being a process you see and may have an influence on)
- Tolerance = I'll endure it ("it" being a process you can't control)
- Indifference = I don't care about an idea or person
- Ambivalence = Uncertainty of how you feel

Words are weapons, if you use the wrong ones you could end up cutting your knees off, or at least hurting your cause. How else can you affect change as a jerk unless you know how to speak? Hopefully, I've driven that point home.

How Confusion Cripples the "Goody-Goodies" but Helps You as a Jerk

Back to helping you become the best jerk, you can be. There is massive human potential. Massive! We are more "connected" than we have ever been; you hear it all the time. We ingest and regurgitate information across the globe at an incredible speed.

If a butterfly flaps its wings in the Amazon, I can watch it on

YouTube! I can watch TikTok or whatever other clock noise apps we're allowed to watch now and spend hours just staring at my phone. I can tweet and tok at the same time, just not while driving. The advertising potential—I mean, the *human* potential is out of this world!

How does this connect to the confusion I've spoken about with the terms of acceptance, tolerance, acknowledgment, and indifference?

On one hand, confusion and indifference sometimes work in our favor. Since everyone is focused on their own situations and lives, the newest technology, the newest TV show. Crisis and causes can be easier to get out in front of or push awareness for out into the world.

However, balls get dropped and communication isn't as straightforward as it should be. That gives an opportunity for us jerks! People don't always speak their minds, and in this day and age, fewer and fewer people speak their minds face to face. Jerk Rule #215!

The world opens up to you in numerous ways if you can manage this. This is Jerk Rule #16: "Not many people can think on their toes, or at least not if you can properly kick their feet out from under them." Sweep that Leg! Cobra Kai!

With all these data points and pieces of information at our fingertips, not only can we look up anything we need whenever we need it, but we also don't have to retain it, because we can just look it up again.

There is a constant reprioritization utilized by companies and people vying for your attention and money. Your attention is also sought after by the media. These aren't new concepts. I'm not blowing your mind by explaining that the media makes money from advertising. It looks for the most sensational stories out there to keep our attention.

There are no conspiracy theories on the higher echelon controlling our lives through media; it's just simple economies of scale at work. That, and the AI algorithms taking over, and our lizard overlords below the ground, or are they above us? I forget. #AllHailSkynet

This vying for attention breaks apart my focus and yours, along with the confusion of what words seem to mean. Not to mention the anxiety of planning for the future while even more people today are drowning in debt or simply fighting to be alive tomorrow.

The prioritization of our socio-economic lives over the fundamentals for all else is a normal concept. Our attention spans are short, things are too complex, and there is no one-size-fits-all solution.

How does the fact that we can't seem to get it together, help me be a better jerk, you ask?

It shows us how we work together. It's messy. Things get forgotten and people feel overwhelmed at times. Confused.

If you can find someone's interest or even direct them to an interest that can be utilized toward a cause, whatever our cause is, we can change things to our liking. As a jerk, that's a selfish goal, but that's why we're here, right? For ourselves.

The problem with motivating people to your cause is that there needs to be a way forward first. That way forward needs to be easier than standing still. If it's not, people will standstill. Not like zombies stand still waiting for the smell of brains. I mean, we have phones... we'll all look down.

As a jerk, this is spectacular news, even with the dark example I laid out. You have the power to mold people to your cause, and you know that people are afraid to speak their minds from all the Twitter tweets. You can get them to buy your junk or play your app, and as long as that's the most interesting thing, the easiest thing, you'll keep their focus.

Bringing it Back Around:
Focusing on Your Cause, Your Jerk Power!

As a jerk in training, you have to figure out what you want people to focus on. Maybe you have a platform already. It's easy nowadays to have one; just sign up on Twitter and start posting. Use Twitch or YouTube or whatever new thing we have out there.

One thing to note, though: as a jerk, you have to have the focus to maintain power. Just like our physics formula requires. If you gain others' focus, you can use it to your benefit, but you have to work for this additional focus and even work overtime to produce the influence necessary to gain more focus. Work is the only path to success, that's not to say others can't work for you!

With additional focus, you have more force to apply to the formula of power. You can't be playing *Words with Friends*, *Clash of Clans*, or *Flappy*

Bird all the time like the other people. You can't worry about "finding yourself" in nature first. Nike had it right—just do it.

Working for success is something we've seemingly failed to convey to some in our society and this has led us to some interesting places. Everything takes work, and to maintain influence you have to work hard for it. Jerk Rule #73, word for word. You must work to steal people's focus and keep it.

If you can't, well, there is no can't. Just know that someone else will.

Standing Up for Yourself vs. Going With the Flow

One more point before we close this final chapter: We discussed how the words we use create confusion, and with so many people all having a different outlook or experience, properly conveying what we mean can be hard. We don't want to ruffle any feathers.

This flows back into the chapter on Fitting In vs. Standing Apart, but it comes full circle here, and I wanted to leave you with this idea. If you are always worried about what others think of what you say, you're not going to have much of a life. Sometimes people don't know what's good for them, and not being a jerk by being quiet, or indifferent can make you a jerk.

Now maybe what you think or say is stupid, but if you never say it, how will you know? #YOLO

Summary

We went over how stupid complex words that people don't understand hurt more than help and are even connected to argumentative fallacies. There are some Jerk Rules to take advantage of that.

This chapter had two major discussion points; we looked at why the terms tolerance and acceptance are complex loaded terms that can stop us from properly engaging with others in a form that could be productive.

Remember, you're not going to change the world in a day, either as a jerk or not. There are people out there who don't believe we can change "the machine" at all. They offer no solutions, only problems.

Since change and world peace are kinda far off, we should probably take advantage of our time as jerks to benefit ourselves, right? Right!

I've gone over how people don't want to discuss certain topics for fear of being attacked. This gives us the advantage. Why? Because as a true jerk, you can't be afraid of what people are going to think of your ideas.

Of course, don't be an idiot, and you'll know quickly enough if you are, but you have to stick your neck out to be a successful jerk. Then again, being indifferent is a great way to become a jerk too!

As jerks, we are in a position to use our awesome power to steal focus and mold this world into what we want it to be, for our benefit. The only question is, what do you want people to focus on?

Jerk Rules

What did you learn?

Jerk Rule #16: Not many people can think on their toes, or at least not if you can properly kick their feet out from under them. Sweep the Leg! Cobra Kai never dies!

Jerk Rule #34: People don't always understand words and won't use them properly. If you can manage that understanding, you can use them to your advantage.

BONUS Jerk Rule #56: Always take the pessimist viewpoint when someone else has an idea, always be the optimist with your own. Don't provide solutions to problems you perceive with others' ideas; it only helps the other opponent... I mean, person. Unless it could help you, then manage that solution closely.
    Pitfall: This could be seen as helping to work out solutions to problems. Be careful of the benefits!

BONUS Jerk Rule #70: Fake research works just as well to influence the masses as real research does. Even the idea of fake research has helped breed confusion! So when in doubt, make it up!

NOT BEING A JERK MAKES YOU A JERK 181

Jerk Rule #73: You must work to steal people's focus, and keep it. If you can't, well, there is no can't. Just know that someone else will.

Pitfall: If you're too smooth, people might gravitate toward you and expect you to perform for them!

Jerk Rule #80: The Middle Ground is the perfect ground! Do what you Wilt! You do you! Jerk Argument Tactic #7 should be applied to life!

Jerk Rule #129: Feelings just get in the way.

Beware the pitfall: Emotions should be the captain of your heart. As a jerk, you should allow your feelings to guide you, but other people's feelings are second fiddle.

Jerk Rule #163: No matter how much we want people to read our minds or seem to think they can, they can't. But you can pretend.

Jerk Rule #215 Many people are afraid to speak their minds and, in this age, even less and less speak their minds face to face. Master good face-to-face communication and the world opens up to you in numerous ways.

Pitfall: Face-to-face conversation can be addicting and you may find you're making actual connections and relationships you care about.

AFTERWORD

ARE YOU A JERK YET? WHAT RULES DO YOU LIVE BY?

I can't accurately gauge what you may have learned. Telling you what you now know sounds like a pretty jerkish thing to do, and since we know I'm a jerk, let's give it a go!

This book lays out skills and qualities people tend to convey and perceive from others. Honestly, I hope you don't want to be a jerk. At least not professionally, like me. I've got enough competition. In pointing these various Jerk Rules out, I hope you glean a new perspective on how the noise of the world might make you forget others.

In this short guide, we've broken up the aspects of who we are, what makes us tick, and why we do some of the things we do. We have only touched the surface of these aspects.

This book wasn't written to make you an expert in who people are or what people think. It was made to give you some introspection on the things you think about yourself, how people see themselves, and other things people don't think about with all the noise around and in us.

If you utilize just one of these tools in your day-to-day, if we've made a difference in one person's life, it was worth it.

In this age of information, with our busy lives wrapped around working and focusing on our futures, we often forget about others, how they see things, and how they feel. We ingest a lot of information and we rarely assess it critically, only to spread it around as truth.

Just because we're doing more for a cause doesn't mean we're getting things done. Research what you stand for, and bring solutions to the table. Otherwise, we're just a bunch of jerks.

Hopefully, this book creates a conversation, maybe even a face-to-face conversation. One that discusses why people do the things they do. Helps you look into other people's smelly shoes.

Why do we talk about things but don't put action behind them? Why waste time pretending? Why do we listen to ideas and accept or reject them purely based on how they make us feel? Why are people sometimes mean to others or harmful to themselves instead of asking for support?

What happens if you directly confront the underlying aspects of someone's angry comments instead of hurling yet another degrading remark? What would happen if we started tracking all the trolls and sent them off to an island to live in isolation with other haters?

Wait… that might not be a good one to delve into. Scratch that. I didn't teach that in the book… I don't think. #TrollTracker2025 #TrollLoJack2050 #IsleOfTheTrolls #TrollHunter2075

All in all, I hope this book makes you think. We don't do that enough these days. We let others think for us because we're too busy, or we're "living our best life now" for those successful ones among us.

We care about people but we don't always have the proper time for them. Let's stop and think about how to get our time back. How can you formulate a plan for yourself and others and argue properly along the way? Let's stop this environment where we're simply being schooled and help each other learn.

We should learn from each other to create a world with rainbows, rhino-horses, and world peace. Or at least some Star Trek-style space travel. Dibs on the red shirt!

We are only in control of our actions in this world. If we start there, maybe—just maybe we can build something better.

Much love in all of your travels,

Alexander D. Loch

BIBLIOGRAPHY

Context is key.
—
Self-Titled Best Selling Author: Alex Loch

Chapter 3 - Self-Esteem and Society:

Weir, Kristen (June 2014, Vol 45, No. 6) "The Lasting Impact of Neglect". American Psychological Association https://www.apa.org/monitor/2014/06/neglect

Hanushek, Jamison, Jamison, and Woessmann (Spring 2008 / Vol. 8, No. 2) "Education and Economic Growth". EducationNext https://www.educationnext.org/education-and-economic-growth/

Chapter 5 - Projecting:

Newcomer, Laura (Sept. 26, 2019) 22 "Standout Groups Stopping Domestic Violence" Greatist https://greatist.com/happiness/stop-domestic-violence-organizations

Wow, are you really reading this?

W.H.O (2020), "Violence Prevention Alliance". World Health Organization https://www.who.int/violenceprevention/participants/en/

Chapter 6 - Ego:
Freud S. (March 22, 2010) *The Ego and Id*. Amazon https://www.amazon.com/Ego-Id-Sigmund-Freud/dp/1451537239

Jung C. G. (Jan. 27, 2003) *The Psychology of the Unconscious*. Amazon https://www.amazon.com/Psychology-Unconscious-C-G-Jung/dp/0486424995

Chapter 7 – What is an Argument?:
Scott, Aaron D. (Nov 17, 2016). "Sorry, But You are Not Entitled to Your Opinion." Medium. https://medium.com/@neallwebster/sorry-but-you-are-not-entitled-to-your-opinion-ef4b06b3f094

Still perusing? Impressive.

Chapter 8 - How to Argue like a Jerk:
Dept of Philosophy (Unknown Date) *Equivocation Fallacy*. Texas State University https://www.txstate.edu/philosophy/resources/fallacy-definitions/Equivocation.html

The Basis for Rule #315 for the "Under" Toilet Paper Position for Jerks:
James, Geoffrey (Aug 8, 2017) "The Correct Way to Hang Toilet Paper, According to Science. Inc." https://www.inc.com/geoffrey-james/the-correct-way-to-hang-toilet-paper-according-to-.html

This one's important.

Chapter 9 - Wielding Power:
Rybczyk, Joseph A. (2016) *Relationship of $E = mc2$ to $F = ma$ and Gravity*. Mr.Relativity.net. https://bit.ly/2UWmRPM

Need help sleeping?

Chapter 10 – Screw Etiquette!:
Doherty, Meghan (Aug 1, 2013) *How Not to be a Dick: An Everyday Etiquette Guide*, Amazon My Book

Give it a try. Could help with the fancy dinners and small talk.

Chapter 11 - Not Being a Jerk Makes You a Jerk:
W.H.O. (Sept 18, 2018) "A Child Under 15 Dies Every 5 Seconds Around the World." World Health Organization https://www.who.int/news-room/detail/18-09-2018-a-child-under-15-dies-every-5-seconds-around-the-world

Need some causes to fight for? Here are some good ones, bigger than words.

Hodal, Kate (Feb 25, 2019) "1 in 200 People is a Slave. Why?" The Guardian https://www.theguardian.com/news/2019/feb/25/modern-slavery-trafficking-persons-one-in-200

I.L.O. (Sept 19, 2017) "Global Estimates of Modern Slavery International Labor Organization" https://www.ilo.org/global/publications/books/WCMS_575479/lang--en/index.htm

APPENDIX

"There are only two perfectly useless things in this world. One is an appendix and the other is Poincaré [politicians]"

—

Georges Eugène Benjamin Clémenceau

Questions For the "non-jerk" or the "better jerk" inside us:

Am I projecting in a conversation?

1. What emotion am I feeling about the conversation or person I just had or am having?
2. Is this feeling warranted, or is something else going on in my life right now?
3. What exactly did they say? What did I say?
4. Am I close with this person, or have we had issues in the past?
5. What might I have done to affect the relationship I have with this person?
6. If I lash out, besides giving me a feeling of "getting back" or "winning," would it help my relationship with them?

7. Can I structure my response to address the issue I see and maintain our relationship?

Capturing Thoughts to Handle Anxiety (Find a Quiet Space)

1. What is the thought?
2. Is it important?
3. Could it have a positive or negative impact on my life if I do or don't ignore it? (Make a note and plan of action for later.)
4. Is it a fun and/or interesting thought? (Write it down or discard it. Repeat this for about 15 minutes. Afterward, you may have a shortlist, a long list, or a jumble of ideas you're not sure where to put.)

Self-Esteem (Jerks Need it, Too!)

1. Do I praise myself for work that is done so-so or perhaps not at all?
2. Do I beat myself up for work that is done well or work that is done so-so?
3. Do I find that I put myself down or blow negative events out of proportion?
4. Do I believe others always need my help, or that I always need help?

The Dos and Don'ts of Projecting Goals

DON'T: Be results-oriented. Focus on the goal. Start working on a plan and then do it.

- How do you feel about being closer to your goal after you finished the day's tasks?

DON'T: Compare yourself to others. Just stop doing it. Jerks don't need to. This is almost without fail a negative comparison.

DO: Compare yourself to who/where you were yesterday. This won't always be positive; you could find you haven't done anything since yesterday, in which case today is the day to start.

However, with this comparison (barring not doing anything), if you are pushing yourself toward a goal, this is almost without fail a positive comparison. I have (whatever I gained) today, and I didn't have it yesterday. I lost this weight today that I had yesterday. Just like self-reliance is positive, this concept of comparison is also.

DO: Remember to work on what you care about. If you don't work on it, don't lie to yourself or put yourself down about not doing something you don't care about. Stop wasting your energy worrying about what you can't control. Focus on the goals you feel you can reach, and reach for them.

DO: Finally, ask for help. Self-reliance does not mean you are supposed to do everything on your own. Self-reliance means you know to ask others for help when you need it. I'm going to stop there or I might just write another book...

ABOUT ALEXANDER DEWEY LOCH AND THE SCHOOL STOPPERS

Alex isn't a real writer with accolades and awards. He has no degrees from MIT nor any bestsellers. If he was just a writer, or Nobel winner, as flesh-and-blood he could be ignored—destroyed, even. No, Alex is more than that.

He's a symbol, incorruptible (apart from his own internal corruption and jerkish flaws). Alex is everlasting. Alex is... the Batman. Er... was I supposed to write something about me here?

Alex Loch is the mouthpiece behind the School Stoppers. While the name may be egregious and not at all suggestive of the writer's true intentions, this make-believe group is willing to climb that uphill battle to make its name ring differently in the hearts and minds of the people that hear it.

For readers will know Alex and the School Stoppers' true goal of promoting and supporting causes that seek education for all, children's health and welfare, and just generally uplifting the economies of the world. As well as getting SpaceX to build the Starship Enterprise, and becoming best friends with Tom Segura and Keanu Reeves.

www.ingramcontent.com/pod-product-compliance
Lightning Source LLC
LaVergne TN
LVHW051519070426
835507LV00023B/3201